Engagement
FOCUS
&TENSION
in
PROJECT
MANAGEMENT

This book is dedicated to Kimbel Nap.

And the beta readers extraordinaire:
Andy Gagnon, Doug Fry, and Dr. Owe Petersen

TABLE OF CONTENTS

1

PRACTICAL PROJECT MANAGEMENT

Let's start with the question: How do I get things done?

The original event prompting the question, "How do things get done?" began in an elective graduate-level project management class. The hope was that what was taught would show a better way to get things done. It turns out other students were there seeking the same enlightenment. A fellow student asked the question first. *How do I get things done?* The formulaic answer from the professor satisfied no one. It was about process, tools, and adhering to the critical path. The disappointment was palpable. The search for a better answer continued.

The next compelling reason for bringing this text into existence came years later. Colleagues and a supervisor complimented the author's workmanlike approach to project management and asked how they could replicate it. Colleagues shared how those unique approaches were seen as successful. Exceptionally difficult tasks, previously seen as impossible to complete, were successfully delivered.

Writing everything down eventually revealed what others were commenting on: A disciplined work style addressing engagement of contributors through knowledge of people-centric phenomena. Subconscious skills addressing more than seventy identified human peculiarities in the project management space. This book is the result.

> The project management in-between space:
> Where people are key to project success

But why take the author's personal notes and expend the considerable effort developing a proper book addressing the topics? **In the hope that others will read it.** If others become aware of what is shared here, their collective professional experience will improve. There was nothing like this when the author began his project management journey. If there had been, so much more could have been accomplished.

A humorous, snarky, more irreverent version, *Streetsmart Project Management,* was written in a memoir style. *Streetsmart* conveyed the concepts of people-centric project management phenomena, but it did so in a way that might not meet professional standards. Acknowledging there are professional environments where colorful language and sarcastic humor are best avoided prompted the development of a second edition of *Streetsmart Project Management.*

Then, something strange happened on the way to publishing

As the more professional second edition of *Streetsmart Project Management* was being finalized, there was a realization. The knowledge of people-centric phenomena has value on its own. But the interconnection between the phenomena was being left undefined. People-centric project management phenomena are governed by other aspects of project management. Engagement, focus, and tension are the tools used (along with the fundamental awareness of the existence of people-centric phenomena) to *get things done. Streetsmart Project Management* became *Engagement, Focus, and Tension in Project Management.*

Who should read this, and what can they expect to learn?

This book is an opportunity to develop skills in the project management space to get things done. There are many project management books available. Presented here is guidance on how people impact project execution. The link between developing tension in a project and leveraging knowledge of people-centric project management phenomena to improve engagement in the project is critical. Managed tension leads to engagement. Engagement is shaped into focus, and focus delivers results.

An apology upfront: There are many phenomena shared in this book. Having a descriptive section for each one makes for a long Table of Contents. To mitigate this burden, they have been moved to an index at the back of the book. Hopefully, this attenuates the dictionary style of phenomena listings.

The art of getting things done

Improving project quality and velocity by incorporating consideration for the human condition into the project management

The art of getting things done is represented by the dozens of skills, strategies, and insights that a project manager uses to improve efficiency, decrease project friction, and more. Those skills, strategies, and insights come from an understanding of an array of interrelated people-centric phenomena. It is not a "list-style" approach, nor a formulaic process.

There is precedent for the possibility of a straightforward, low-cost effort delivering dramatic productivity gains. As an example, the advance in technology improving getting things done, is the use of two computer monitors instead of one. A 30%+ increase in productivity can be expected from adding a second monitor. No training, no increase in headcount, no updating of a process. A negligible investment resulting in productivity increases rivaling expectations from a major capital investment.

For details on the above productivity numbers, perform an internet search for Jon Peddie Research, Robert Dow, and dual monitors.

It is speculated here that a similarly productivity-enhancing opportunity can be found in acknowledging people-centric project management phenomena and working to develop skills and strategies leveraging them.

This book is the self-help opportunity to master people-centric project management phenomena and achieve improvements in quality and project velocity with minimal investment.

By addressing the people-centric phenomenon in the project management space, there is an opportunity to roll up your sleeves and get your hands dirty in the engine of project management by making things happen and getting things done.

No homework will be assigned

A glossary of terms, notes on organization, a quick-start reading guide, and an index of people-centric phenomena can be found at the end of this book.

A variety of practical and applied approaches to project management are presented throughout this book. However, there will be no Gantt or

PERT charts, nor formulaic spreadsheet tools. This book is also checklist-free.

There are, however, a few descriptions of phenomena for which a solution is elusive. Confirmation that they exist provides the reader the opportunity to plan for them.

Not profession-dependent

There is no particular role, experience, or education level associated with what is presented here. This book is intended for a broad range of skills experiences, and professions. Whenever there is an attempt to accomplish a task, and human beings are involved, there are opportunities for improvement.

Although the cover of the book says, "Project Management," the insights shared within are universal. Project management happens whenever someone attempts a task in an organized manner. The ideas and concepts shared throughout the book are universally applicable and deliver value for any project. Whether rebuilding your car's suspension or improving project teamwork across a global corporation, everyone engages in project management.

2

PROJECT MANAGEMENT & PEOPLE

What does a project manager do? While this scope may not be determined by the reader, it is possible to provide some structure around such a general statement.

People, process, and prioritization matter.
— Andy Gagnon

In the first chapter of this book, it was stated this book would not contain lists. That was partially true. There are bullet point lists shared, like the one below, of what might be expected of a project manager:

- **Communicate**
- **Provide focus and clarity**
  - What are we doing?
  - When will it be done?
  - And sometimes, what we will *not* be doing*
- **Engage and organize**
  - Contributors
  - Information
  - Resources
- **Provide leadership**

- o Consistency
- o Planning
- o Strategy
- o Positivity
- **Run interference**

The above bullet points do not represent an exhaustive list. (*) The bullet point indicating what will not be getting done usually gets some attention. What is meant by *what is not to be done?* Most project managers talk about what is to be accomplished, not what isn't. The do-not-do list could be essentially infinite. They can't all be named. However, there are specific unconstructive avenues of effort that may be appealing to a contributor(s). These alternate paths to apply bandwidth need to be proactively walled off.

> Critical thinking is the process of using information to make logical, well-thought-out judgments and decisions.

Actualizing communications, focus and clarity, organization, and leadership require critical thinking skills. There will be many opportunities over the course of a project to use these skills.

All projects exist to create value.

All projects exist to increase or create value. Resources and labor hours are organized as inputs, with a defined output chartered as the goal. Between those inputs and outputs is a vast interaction of human activity. People, communication, and process—this in-between space that is the focus of *Engagement, Focus, and Tension in Project Management.*

Engagement in projects

Many leaders in project management start a process, prompt an action, or provide instruction, and then expect that the contributor(s) involved will continue the process without distraction. This is not how the real world works. People get distracted or bored. People are assigned elsewhere. A contributor reaches a point where they can't continue without further instructions. The list of potential project speed bumps here is infinite. Without attention from the project manager, the project may cease to progress for lack of direction. This is where engagement from the project manager is needed. A manager must stay engaged to prevent delays.

Engagement is a broad concept in project management. It includes building teams of contributors, soliciting experts, and keeping the project on track. Engagement means regular follow-ups with the many people supporting the project. The needed engagement must evolve beyond requesting status updates. Certain tasks and people will have differing needs of engagement energy. There is no scripted approach that captures the how or when of engagement. Knowing engagement is required across the aspects of the project is a first step. Navigating the people-centric project management phenomena is perhaps a second step. The customizing of engagement based on individual people and project characteristics is the final bit of wisdom shared here.

Focus in projects

What are we doing today? What are we doing tomorrow? Which task is first? How will each day's distractions be resolved? Who is doing what? Who will determine the answers to these questions? Here is where the project manager delivers focus.

Having contributors interfacing with a project is important. What is even more important is focused work to achieve project goals. The right work at the right time in the appropriate sequence. This will not happen without focus. Communication, tools, and energy must have definition and discipline with a goal. Organizing contributor engagement and resources in pursuit of project objectives. This is the focus a project manager provides. Making sure the correct activities occur completely and in the correct order. This focus cannot be in the project manager's head. It must be messaged to the team. This messaging must use language the team is comfortable with. One of this book's largest chapters addresses project management communications. Keeping contributors focused requires excellent communication skills.

A curious aspect of focus is the occasional need to define what should be excluded. Keeping out the things that disturb or outright prevent project focus. While working with the project's focus messaging, it may become obvious there are contributors who wish to do more. If this more is not explicitly excluded, effort may be wasted on unasked-for output.

Tension in projects

Tension is a complicated word that is prone to misunderstanding or mischaracterization. In the context of engagement and focus, tension is about a sense of urgency and visibility. This tension influences the likelihood that the project stays a priority for project contributors.

Managing project tension benefits from understanding how people engage with different project activities. Copying a senior manager in an email injects tension for the recipient. An impromptu hallway run-in can be leveraged to add tension with some basic questions or the sharing of project activities. Injecting tension can be achieved by a straightforward text requesting an update.

Tension can be introduced, maintained, or increased. Introducing tension is often associated with a beginning, the start of something that is not a continuation from a previous effort. Maintaining tension is about keeping the subconscious visibility to the project's process. If the appropriate level of tension is already in effect, then a minimal level of contact is still needed to prevent loss of tension.

A project manager may discover contributors are not engaging and an increase in tension is warranted. Perhaps a meeting must be called or a member of leadership requested to lean in. The goal is to prompt engagement and maintain focus.

Not everyone requires the same level of tension to respond. There are many who pick up on the barest wisp of introduced tension. Others may require a raised voice to get the point across. Figuring out what level is needed is a skill that improves with practice. Positive tension can generate positive engagement. This enthusiasm is a desired outcome that can improve project velocity and quality. Creating and maintaining positive tension is difficult. Tension is also easily abused. A straightforward reasoning process may conclude that if a little is good, then more must be better; therefore, they maximize output by increasing tension to the maximum. Bullying increases tension, and there are those who leverage barking, intimidation, and threats to people as part of their tension toolbox. The downside to these negative styles is that they kill initiative, creativity, and quality. Especially when overdone to the point where the target knows that nothing they do will meet the requirement. If the highest value outcome is desired, a proportional and positively applied tension is the only way to achieve success.

A negative tension situation occurs when competing interests fight over scarce resources prompting them to engage in a tension-escalating battle. The contributors caught in the middle will not appreciate this and project outcomes are more likely to be negatively impacted.

What are people-centric project management phenomena?

When working on a project, has something unexpected caught your attention? Mostly related to people being involved? Maybe the project comes under overly detailed scrutiny? Perhaps emails seem to go in circles? Are there strange, peculiar, or even downright weird situations that are difficult to explain? Then on the next project these strange people things happen again. This time you notice it right away.

While you are working on another project, there are the subtle signs that those eccentric people events are going to occur again. And then they do. These are people-centric project management phenomena.

People-centric project management phenomena are repeated human actions influencing a project's outcomes. The first step in understanding these phenomena is exposure to the idea that they exist. This insight begins the self-help journey.

> Learning of the existence of people-centric project management phenomena and developing skills to leverage that knowledge is perhaps as much a journey as a destination.

Many of the people-centric phenomena are part of the engagement, focus, and tension equation. Some phenomena support improved project execution and are to be encouraged. Many phenomena complicate or outright hinder project activities. These repeating, quirky, poorly understood characteristics are common to almost every project management effort. Regardless of geography, culture, or profession, they involve themselves, for good or bad, in projects everywhere.

There is more to consider, other poorly defined influences that increase project friction and interrupt the critical path. People-centric events injecting additional delays and complexity, thereby slowing project execution. Over time, it becomes apparent these people-centric anomalies are not the exception. There are many different phenomena, and they are repeatable to the point of being predictable.

The above observation leads to the déjà vu aspect of phenomena and a questioning realization: *Am I the only one seeing this?* The understanding that something unconstructive is recurring during project execution is perhaps not déjà vu in the traditional sense but instead an all too familiar obstacle. Repeated observation of these similar and interrelated phenomena impacting project execution performance leads to the understanding that they are real and not figments of a frustrated project manager's imagination. The source of these odd, repeatable situations is mostly the same: people. Not necessarily in a malicious way, it is just people being people. The descriptions introduced here establish a common reference for these observed events: the people-centric phenomena. This understanding leads to the need to categorize and define what has been observed. Once defined, strategies can be formulated to address the phenomenon in the future.

> The common understanding that people-centric phenomena exist is uncommon.

Over time, and as project efforts are executed, numerous individual phenomena will reveal themselves. They are a common experience regardless of company, country, language, or geography. Achieving better project outcomes through improved soft skills, best practices, lessons learned, and common understanding.

People-centric project management phenomena are real.

Most of the phenomena have been given colorful names. Partially to make them memorable, also because of the thoughts inspired when experiencing them.

One final note about people-centric phenomena: Many of them are not rational. Meaning they do not make sense why anyone is doing them. Regardless, they exist.

Engagement, focus, tension, and people-centric project management phenomena are interrelated

Engagement is used to deliver tension. Tension and engagement maintain focus. Focus makes sure the project achieves its goals and nothing else

People-centric project management phenomena are artifacts of, or interrelated to, the engagement, tension, and focus trifecta. Managing phenomena requires awareness and mastery of engagement, focus, and tension.

All four of those project management characteristics require communication skills. Communication skills maximize engagement and focus messaging, while also tuning tension.

How to start or the path forward:

- Communication skills
- Engagement, focus, tension
- People-centric project management phenomena

13

But how to engage phenomena? Is there a suggested process? Yes, that is where PIML comes into play.

Prevent, Ignore, Mitigate, or Leverage (PIML)

The basic actions that can be taken with phenomena are to Prevent, to Ignore, to Mitigate, or to Leverage. PIML for short.

Prevent: This is to acknowledge the precursors to a people-centric phenomenon occurrence and to take action to end it before it happens. Prevent could also be Predict. As familiarity with phenomena increases, so does the ability to predict when they are going to happen and act to prevent them. Engage contributors early and communicate what is needed to prevent or leverage the phenomena.

Ignore: This is an option when just knowing what is happening allows for compensation to prevent any undesirable impact on project execution. Instead of falling into a phenomenon trap, the project manager manages around it.

Mitigate: This is required when a phenomenon is occurring and must be addressed. This situation is the most difficult to mediate, as there is often little warning and the other people involved are the source of the challenge. Engage with the relevant stakeholders and elevate visibility of what is happening. Move quickly to preserve the focus on project elements that might be impacted. Inject tension as needed to motivate contributors to avoid or to resolve any challenges.

Leverage: Not all people-centric phenomena are negative. There are some that can be leveraged. This leveraging is how a project manager can deliver unexpected success.

WHAT DO YOU MEAN, NOBODY KNOWS WHAT'S GOING ON?

An interesting first engagement, focus, and tension-related people-centric project management phenomenon to be shared: Not everyone is aware they exist. Experienced project managers will recognize many of the engagement, focus, and tension aspects of project management. They also will nod in understanding as they read the people-centric phenomenon. But few have linked them all together and woven that understanding into their project efforts.

This is the challenge of this phenomenon. Once the reader understands, they will benefit. But there is even more benefit if others are enlightened. Then true synergy can be realized.

This realization, that there are things undiscovered and unexplained, is the first step in a journey to realizing this also applies to the project management human equation. There are unknowns as to why people do what they do. These poorly understood human behaviors have real-world implications. And project management is a very human endeavor.

IT'S REALLY NOT INTUITIVE

Experienced project managers will recognize some, or even many, of the phenomena presented here. However, an unanticipated outcome is just how many of them exist.

People-centric project management phenomena are not intuitive.

The understanding of phenomena and the skills to address them are not intuitive or commonly understood, nor is understanding them developed on its own. Without help from others, many people will not "just figure it out." Neither the realization of the existence of the phenomena nor the skills needed to address the phenomena develop without guidance.

Executing improved project performance through engagement, focus, and tension is also not intuitive. Crude forms of applying tension are well known. The way tension works is not.

Below are the three personal stories that introduced the author to the concept of people-centric project management phenomena—a journey to that moment when the realization there was more became too obvious to ignore:

> While attending a Society of Women Engineers (SWE) meeting, two colleagues at least twenty years apart in age went to lunch together. Project management was the first topic brought up in conversation. The youngest of the two shared their confusion and frustration regarding the ever-changing priorities and the havoc it was causing.

> Having already identified this as a common phenomenon, the senior of the two shared *the ABCDE incidence* concept detailed later in this book. Explaining that this is something that happens often in project management, a straightforward demonstration on a paper napkin was drawn up. A short and to-the-point example.

> The junior colleague appreciated the explanation, glad for the insight and confirmation they are not the only person

seeing the problem. A photo of the ABCDE scribbles was taken along with a thank you given for sharing.

A takeaway from this experience was the realization people-centric observations about project management phenomena were real and could be useful.

* * * * *

In another instance, a supervisor, after a year of managing a direct report's work observed their workman-like approach and effectiveness in executing and completing projects. One colleague even started referring to the project manager as the "sledgehammer" for their success in moving difficult projects forward. This individual was implementing engagement, focus, and tension techniques from their "toolbox." The same toolbox shared in this book delivered tangible results—and real value for their employer.

Another colleague commented on the author's project management style. It was pointed out that while executing a project, many of the actions taken were not intuitive to those watching. Then at some point, the project would come together successfully at the end. Frustratingly, the process was not clear to a casual observer. This was the result of acknowledging people-centric project management phenomena strategies in project planning. And then navigating them successfully through engagement, focus, and tension.

These experiences led to the conclusion there is an opportunity in developing a set of project management tools. The result is a toolbox providing colleagues and leadership additional insight into mutually experienced challenges. This toolbox establishes an opportunity for synergy in a collective understanding.

> Synergy is delivered through a collective understanding of people-centric project management phenomena.

Explaining engagement, focus, and tension (EFT) and project management phenomena to colleagues or management is not a straightforward activity. The concepts shared here may violate long-standing practices, and pointing out the problem is not a path to endearing oneself to others. Alerting a colleague that they practice one of the phenomena presented in this book may not have a positive outcome. Do not expect it to be easy nor that your colleagues will quickly buy into the concept. But attenuating the influence of these phenomena is worth it.

3

PROJECT COMMUNICATION

Project management involves communicating with numerous people over a variety of channels. These communications include impromptu one-on-one chats or presentations to a large group. The need to exchange information is constant. Let's take a moment to clarify two aspects of communication shared here: The first is the ability to understand and communicate the existence of people-centric phenomena. The second is the unique nature of project management communications. The short burst of exchange, soliciting information or prompting action. These are different communication opportunities, both of which are covered in this chapter. Introduced here are communication-related phenomena and soft skill recommendations for improving communication. Communication is how engagement is achieved, and without this first step, it is impossible to improve engagement, focus, and tension and to navigate people-centric project management phenomena.

The author executed a Lean Six Sigma Green Belt project. For the final storyboard presentation, a slide was shown with the names of everyone associated with the project. By going back and reviewing meeting requests, emails, and project documentation, a list could be constructed. The total was thirty-five contributors engaged. The breadth and depth of project communication are often underestimated.

> Communication is a tool serving a purpose, and like other tools, it must be used properly.

The ability to communicate is a basic building block of civilization. It is so fundamental and pervasive that perhaps too little thought is given to improving daily communication quality, written or spoken. Does the reader believe there is room for improvement in their daily written and verbal communications? If so, how will improvement be measured? How can the gaps be identified?

Perhaps the first step is to accept there can be improvement. Next is the self-evaluation looking for the gaps. Then, after taking action to improve, measuring the improvement, and then planning subsequent action.

There are numerous opportunities to improve communication quality in the project management environment. Proper structure, getting to the point, using the correct language, and more. Improvements in these spaces reduce contributor bandwidth consumption and decrease errors.

A peculiar type of project management communication is the future planned discussion. This is a note on the calendar to reach out to a specific person or group on a particular day. The message is known days, or even months, ahead of time. It just needs to wait for the right time.

How is communication quality measured? Perhaps in the shortening of the length of an email while maintaining equal content? The rare capturing of the complete message in a single exchange? Limiting the number of participants to the minimum needed to achieve the desired outcome?

There is no shortage of opportunity in this space.

WHAT WE HAVE HERE IS A FAILURE TO COMMUNICATE...

If two people witnessed the same phenomenon at the same time, could they explain it to each other?

A common language is a requirement.

The principles shared in this book can be difficult to express in casual conversation. These insights into project complexity are challenging to explain quickly, a likely scenario when deadlines are looming.

Communication Challenge:

1. People-centric communication phenomena exist.

2. Communicating an occurrence in real-time is problematic.

Shared frustration is the typical outcome when working through commonly recurring project management phenomena that are, paradoxically, not commonly understood. This frustration drives the need for a record of concepts and situations that can be shared to create a **common language**.

There's a compelling need for a common language of project management people-centric phenomena—even if it is only local to your organization. Terms and definitions everyone agrees on. Communication phenomena are complex and counterintuitive. This is the genesis of the idea of this book as a tool. The physical copy of the book is an instrument of clarification to identify shared challenges in project management and provide a path to resolution. If two people have read it, they can reference it when their shared project demonstrates one of the phenomena described.

This supports colleagues developing a common project management language for complex project management phenomena. Having a reference leads to resolution of project management phenomena and misunderstandings, improved engagement, and ultimately, better project delivery.

IT ALL WENT HORRIBLY WRONG

Even if two people are familiar with a people-centric phenomenon event, what words can they use to describe it? Quick, recognizable terms would be the most desirable. This observed phenomenon is the recurrence of common people-centric phenomena without names and definitions associated with them. How can contributors address the situation if they do not share a common language? They need to have read and thought about the phenomena ahead of time. Again, this is due to the non-intuitive nature of these phenomena.

To aid in collaboration, each chapter and phenomenon described herein has a relatable, and sometimes humorous, title to aid in recalling topics. From this structure, the hope is communication about the difficult-to-explain phenomena can be efficiently achieved.

The goal is to prevent misunderstandings of what are likely regular challenges.

Communication Is Fundamental

There are only four ways to know someone: by what they say, what they write, their appearance, and what they do. This is an abbreviated explanation but delivers the point.

> A peculiarity of project management communications is that they are often brief.

Project management involves resources, planning, goals, deliverables, and more. All of this must be communicated verbally and in writing. Without effective, organized, and strategic communication, a project manager will never reach their potential.

Now add the global environment to the communications equation. Long-term collaboration and relationships are often initiated and maintained without ever meeting in person. English as a second language, different cultures, and time zones are all part of a communication environment with limited personal contact.

Verbal and written communications in today's hyperconnected workplace have multiple dimensions that need to be considered. It is not unusual to have a phone conversation or email exchange between contributors who have never (nor will ever) meet in person. The collaborative effort is often. executed exclusively through impersonal forms of communication. In this communication environment, a robust, polished communication skill set will deliver superior project management outcomes.

What effort has the reader applied to improving their verbal or written communications effectiveness? Examples:

- Soliciting feedback on phone style and effectiveness
- Sensitivity to removing the dreaded "I" or "you"
- Is there an easily perceived point to the communication?
- Is there superfluous wording and chatter?
- Emails following an easy-to-read format?
- Performed a self-reflection on communication capabilities?

As communication skills are developed, combining different communication concepts further improves the likelihood of achieving the desired outcome. Eventually, proficiency delivers comfort with dynamic, real time implementation of different approaches.

> Developing a structured, practiced approach to communications reduces the time spent communicating.

Communication is not just the mechanical act of transferring information through a chosen medium. Other considerations include the timing of the communication, carefully considered words, tone, who is included or excluded in the copy, the information transferred, and the action prompted.

Demeanor and attitude will impact the effectiveness of communications. A positive attitude, especially in the face of adversity, is a force multiplier in achieving your goals. Remaining consistently calm and positive demonstrates maturity as a project manager.

> Clear, concise communications using the same structure every time conditions the

> consumer to find what they need more
> quickly.

Communication is a complex endeavor, and acknowledging this is a critical insight. Some few people are natural communicators. For the rest of us mere mortals, we must work at it.

Communications achieves its highest effectiveness by considering one of the more misunderstood professions: sales. The development of long-term customer relationships. The complexities of a supplier/customer interaction. Cold-calling and more. The sales effort is conducted almost exclusively in the communication space.

Sales communications are complex. Done correctly, it is like having a superpower. Alternatively, communications that miss the mark could turn a difficult situation into a firestorm of failure. Well-developed communication skills can turn a deteriorating situation into the building block of mutual future success—especially when engaging different professions within an organization.

Individuals bring certain skills and experience to the work environment.

Different professions have their own "language."

Communication is an everyday requirement in project management. Project management is an exercise in communication and human interaction. Perhaps more so than in being proficient in whatever computer programs or tools an organization subscribes to.

Communication details to consider prior:

➔ Think about what you will say.

➔ Think about what you will write.

No one appreciates reading or listening to a meandering, unfocused statement or question.

- Think about what is to be shared.
- Say it.
- And then **stop**.

Communicate at the optimum time. In meetings, there is a benefit to waiting, letting others share first. This helps to better understand the progression of the discussion and give others the space to talk. People are compelled to talk, and it is often best to let them get it out. This is just part of the human equation. Then, at the end of the meeting, engage and deliver a final message before the meeting ends. This final message is the most likely one to be remembered.

> Timing plays a role in communications.

Consistency in communication is important. There is value in speaking and writing in a repeatable way. This predictability will eventually help others minimize the time to get the needed information.

> Try reading what you wrote out loud.

One technique for learning more about the quality of a written message is to try reading it out loud to another person.

Let's focus on this concept: *A repeated, predictable form of written communication minimizes the amount of time and effort needed for the recipient to understand.*

If time spent on understanding could be reduced by 1% in a large global organization, the cost savings would be impressive. For continuous improvement-oriented individuals, developing communication skills is a never-ending source of beneficial growth.

Building Bridges

Cultivating relationships with colleagues is a critical skill. Most endeavors involve people. People require relationships. Building bridges is foundational to establishing constructive relationships. To survive, to develop, and to excel in the project management environment requires a network of colleagues to provide support. Be prepared to engage both laterally and vertically across the organization (and outside the organization) when building bridges. Perhaps a key person in a different time zone is needed, or someone in shipping and receiving. Projects can have broad elements requiring enterprise-wide collaboration.

Bridge-building success will hinge on a singular characteristic: *Credibility*. The more developed the reputation as a good-faith partner, the more likely others will engage for mutual success. Professional relationships are mutually beneficial. This is not a one-way engagement. This is where the qualities of politeness and professionalism deliver. Be personable. Be useful. Be able to present a mutually beneficial value proposition in a way that is easily understood.

Building Bridges eventually evolves to the next level: networking. Engage colleagues from across the organization. Organizational networking is a next-level project management demonstration of skill. Look at the organization chart. Be prepared to operate outside an immediate cocoon of colleagues. Think about how to introduce yourself to others. A reasonable conclusion is that building bridges is a calculating and manipulative approach. Yes, it is. Project management is all about planning, calculating, positioning resources, and leveraging every opportunity to achieve success, all while adhering to the organization's policies and maintaining your integrity.

There is much focus on planning, process, and tools in project management. Determining the critical path, achieving on-time delivery, and delivering below budget are a few examples. *Building Bridges* is the adjacent requirement for procedural and technical success. The people-centric side of project management requires just as much calculation and consideration. Make *Building Bridges* part of your sophisticated project management "people plan." It cannot be emphasized enough how important *Building Bridges* is. This is a critical success factor for career development. Develop this skill until it is a reflex.

Asking Good Questions

Here is another form of engagement. It is also a method for applying tension. People pay attention when asked a question. They wonder what the real goal is. Asking questions is a superpower on par with the use of silence. Some questions are straightforward requests for singular, obvious, and defined information. The goal in these requests is a fast and efficient process for all parties involved. Other requests are more along the lines of troubleshooting. The goal being to solicit unknowns and find solutions.

> Asking an efficient, organized, to-the-point question, is a skill.

A software developer found that if he posted a request for assistance on a software forum, he either did not get any answer or someone purposefully posted the wrong answer just to be inflammatory. In some cases, the denizens of the internet took this opportunity to deliver insults.

The magic happened when he purposely posted an incorrect interpretation, essentially playing dumb. Then the denizens of the internet could not provide the correction fast enough.

Ask an incorrect question to get corrected—people love to point out when someone is wrong—use this to get info quickly.

There are times when an answer is required and an imperfect and obviously incorrect interpretation of the situation is purposefully shared with the greater team. Basically, broadcasting the asker's ignorance. Most people see this as an admission of weakness. Except this will trigger others to provide a correction. Some are doing this to genuinely help. Others get a shot of superiority from correcting you. **The needed information to move the project forward is delivered in record time.** Build up some credibility before trying this. This approach is not something to execute during the first week on a new job.

The profession of the question's recipient will impact how the question is structured. Engineers will interpret and respond differently than those in marketing. There are no hard and fast rules for navigating these engagements, other than being aware of the differences and that each communication is unique and dynamic.

In advance, an apology to the engineers who read this. The goal is not to single out the profession, but what is shared here is true. Engineers love tech and gadgets and talking about them. Engineers revel in expounding on their respective areas of expertise. Ask a few questions to get the conversation started, then sit back and nod occasionally. Sporadically ask encouraging questions and practice active listening. The value shared will flow faster than most are able to write it down.

Key insight: Technical specialists with knowledge deep and wide are often challenged when answering questions from anyone outside their profession. Many of them gave up years ago explaining to the uninitiated what they do. It is not that they are antisocial or unwilling. Their understanding of specific technical environments is so rare that outside of a peer, it is unlikely anyone who asks a question regarding their specialty will ever understand. This may result in a situation where if a question is asked of a technical expert, the answer may not make sense to someone not immersed in the same subject matter. The lack of

29

common ground makes understanding each other almost impossible. The questioner lacks the understanding to pose a proper question, and the subject matter expert is challenged to provide an answer the listener will understand. **Though technical experts are proficient in the unique aspects of their profession, their expertise in communicating this expertise has not benefitted from the same level of development.** Be mindful of this situation when engaging experts. The question may have to be presented in different ways, coming at it from different directions until a bridge of common understanding is constructed. Often, this feels like an IQ test combined with a patience marathon. This skill improves with experience.

Then there are the questions soliciting an unknown. There are times a question results in a colleague commenting, "Just look it up on the internet or read the manual." Why might basic questions be asked regardless of simplicity or readily available internet answers?

Because there is context and experience needed for a proper answer. Things that are not written down. By asking the expert, a door opens to the possibility for a more complete and sophisticated answer than will be found on the internet or in a manual.

Often when asking a question, the receiver will counter-request: why is the question being asked? Perhaps they do this out of genuine curiosity. Maybe they think the action the question is leading to is a bad idea. Others are perhaps looking for leverage. How badly is an answer needed? Perhaps this is an opportunity for some form of transaction.

Replying to a question with a question may result in unintended consequences. Why? Because instead of a straightforward question-answer transaction, it can lead to further discussion and then work and action items. Or worse, a science project to go looking for even more answers. The receiver of the original question now has work they did not have before the question was posed to them.

There is value in answering questions
quickly and completely.

Questions have a purpose, and out of respect for the person being asked, make the question concise. The recipient of the question should understand it. Clear language, no ambiguous wording—**the goal is no ambiguous requests**. This is partially achieved through due diligence. Figure out as much as possible without burdening colleagues.

The goal is no ambiguous requests.

Minimizing risk and asking good questions are an important combination as well. Do not ask without confirming it is safe to do so. Ask if there is a reason for why things are the way they are. Do not start taking actions before the complete picture is clear. Sometimes, a situation is as intended, even if it appears somewhat incongruous.

Avoid delivering risk along with a
question.

Answering questions often has risk associated with it. The receiver will be responsible for the quality and negative outcomes of the information shared. Narrowly focused questions reduce this risk and make it more likely an answer will be provided.

Now Can You Explain It?

Adjunct professor at an engineering school is a challenging role. Teaching reveals how thoroughly a subject is understood. This understanding becomes apparent after spending several hours in preparation for each hour of instruction. The instructor spends more time studying in preparation than the students and then endures poorly conceived questions from his students. The teacher needs skill to provide clear explanations for unclear questions.

Word choices, context, and completeness all need to be considered when answering questions. Language skills, education, and experience of the recipient are important factors. One approach is to review an explanation from the recipient's point of view.

> Consider your explanation from the viewpoint of the person you are communicating to. If you received your explanation, would you understand what is being said?

Let's say that again: *Consider your explanation from the viewpoint of the person you are communicating to. If you received your explanation, would you understand what is being said?*

In this instant message, email, and information-overload age, incomplete communication is common. Ill-thought-out responses and rushed word choices deliver less than constructive outcomes. In the international setting, explanations require genuine effort as English as a second language comes into play. Americans must stop using slang and pop culture references. Cease using vague, non-specific words such as "thing," "stuff," "sorta," etc.

Explanations are a skill to be developed. Time and money are saved by quality explanations. Delivering an on-target message that resonates with the recipient, constitutes a complete answer, and does not require additional clarification is a beautiful thing.

IN PERSON FOR MAXIMUM EFFECT

How to achieve maximum engagement, focus, and tension for minimal investment? Do it in person.

Introverts (e.g., Myers-Briggs Type Indicator INTJ) are by nature not likely to engage others in person. Their natural inclination is to avoid developing in-person communication effectiveness. This avoidance is a challenge to overcome.

In-person verbal communication is most influential and effective. Alternatively, other verbal communication (phone, internet) is better than written. Email and instant messaging are the worst for connecting and prompting action. Choose the channel based on the desired outcome.

If a fast response is the goal, in-person is the priority. Walk over to another's workspace and start up that conversation. Alternatively, pick up the phone and make a call before resorting to email or instant messaging.

WORDS MATTER

Have you ever been talking to someone and their word choices make you cringe? Or witnessed someone tell the director the approach being suggested is stupid? Word choices can make or break engagement efforts. An appropriate word choice can deliver the right amount of tension. Language directly impacts the clarity of communications.

Yes, this people-centric project management phenomenon, *Words Matter*, counts.

People react to word choices used. This is one of many possible examples: "Just tell me what I need to know" versus "Is there guidance that can be shared on the path forward?"

Other, less-than-constructive communication approaches:

◊ **Making it personal:** "You" as in "Are you done yet?"
◊ **Negative style:** "How many times must this be requested?"

When making word choices, always lean towards positive and neutral. If it feels confrontational, inflammatory, or insinuative to the writer, it is almost guaranteed to be received that way. A single poor or inflammatory word choice can ruin the message.

Examples, unconstructive » constructive:

- Do you have this information? » Would you have visibility to this information?

- It is a simple request. » This should be a straightforward request.

- Can you tell me how to do this? » Is there guidance available on the path forward?

- Are you done yet? » Is there visibility to the completion date?

- When will you be done? -> Has the completion date been determined?

- My day is acceptable. » I am having a fantastic day.

An experienced sales manager, he shared some profound advice. He said to never use the word "simple." Use "straightforward," "my understanding is," or even "basic," but never "simple." He said that if something is described as "simple" and the person being addressed does not understand immediately, you have insulted them for not understanding the "simple" concept.

An even more skilled approach is to avoid words that may be negatively interpreted and instead deliver a more collaborative message, such as, "Would it be possible for us to work together to solve this challenge?"

Words having a common meaning does not prevent a situation-dependent interpretation from arriving at an undesired outcome. Unintended word interpretation may seem over-represented here but over time, word choices will be seen as having an impact.

Observe and practice to become familiar with certain inflammatory words ("simple" is one). Eventually these words stand out when reading and writing them. This visibility creates the opportunity to navigate around them. The effect of word choice in communications is often situation-dependent, and decisions need to be made dynamically during a conversation.

Sensitivity to word choices is important when developing a particular topic's messaging. Word selection and audience awareness will make the difference between a message influencing the desired outcome versus a message missing the mark. This concept could be one of the reasons why marketing and communication careers exist.

Beneficial word choices deliver constructive tension to the communication. Less constructive word choices still deliver tension. But perhaps not the best tension for the situation. Again, awareness and practice will help develop this skill.

FORTY-THREE SECONDS

While visiting customers with an experienced sales manager (the same individual as in the *Words Matter* example), an insight was shared. "Forty-three seconds," he said. "You only get forty-three seconds to deliver your message. Anything longer and you will lose them, or what you are saying may not be interpreted in the way you intended."

Everyone has sat through a meeting where the presentation feels unending. The message shared by the speaker(s) is difficult to determine with over-emphasis on tangential details, gets sidetracked, and never pauses to allow others to participate. A skilled summary of the entirety of what was shared is only three sentences. Enduring the forty minutes of presentation was unnecessary. Quantity is not quality.

But why is this a phenomenon? Because it is not intuitive despite being incredibly effective. If a comment, request, or statement cannot be verbalized in forty-three seconds, go back and work on it.

Think about the message. Get to the point. Do not go off on tangents. Add no filler. Do not try to impress anyone. Just drill the message and stop.

Alternatively stated: Deliver the key points followed by a couple of sentences providing details, **then shut up.** Pardon the blunt language, but knowing when to stop talking is a skill. Acknowledge this and build the ability to deliver a concise message with a clear ending.

Ideally, this concept of *Forty-Three Seconds* should become THE global communications mantra.

SPEAK THE LANGUAGE

There is a Bible story about an attempt to build a tower to heaven (the Tower of Babel). God eventually cast the tower down, dooming humanity to speak many languages instead of one, thus preventing another heaven-reaching attempt from ever occurring again. Communicating in the modern work environment often feels like the delivery of this judgment.

There are so many professions and specialties, each with its own unique jargon or terminology. Engaging finance or engineering (or any other company department) without considering profession-dependent language is not a winning communication strategy. Approaching project management in a profession-centered way is not constructive. Respecting other professions and their contributions to the collective effort is a necessity.

An employer tasked an engineer with managing the North American marketing and communications efforts. This had them working with a proper marketing firm on advertising, trade shows, publications, and announcements.

The marketing firm's people were talented and competent. The marketing account manager sought input from the engineer on something with significant artistic content. They were seeking confirmation that what had been shared looked is acceptable.

The response: "You're asking me? This is your area of expertise. What is your call on this?" Their understanding of the ask was sufficient to realize the firm should rely on others more skilled for input. In this case, it was the people working at the firm.

Project management will have you interacting with other professions and groups within the organization. Engineers talking to marketing people. Accountants in finance collaborating with business professionals on budgets. Each of these professions has different professional languages. Accountants and engineers tend to be structured and introverted. Marketers and salespeople tend to be extroverted and organizationally creative. Use the words they value when speaking to them. Even the smallest amount of this insight will go a long way toward improving project execution when contributors are needed from different backgrounds.

In addition to learning how to better engage colleagues by taking into consideration the unique language of their chosen profession, it is also important to not inflict the project manager's chosen profession's more eccentric approaches to communication. Adapt your language depending on the audience. It can help prevent painful misunderstandings.

Often, projects include broad lateral and vertical elements. Negotiating this labyrinth requires sophisticated and professional communication skills. Project managers will likely interact with different professions, skills, experiences, and levels of engagement. Subject-matter experts with a high degree of skill in a unique specialty may be involved. This spectrum of partners requires skill and sensitivity to engage successfully. Organizing and executing a project across departments and involving different professions requires a practical and practiced approach.

Hence, there comes the need to develop the skills and practice engaging the Tower of Babel that is project management.

LEFT BRAIN VERSUS RIGHT BRAIN

One side of the brain is focused on math, reasoning, problem-solving, and logic. The other side is where communication, art, and similar skills reside. Individuals typically have a dominant side. Engineers often begin on the math and logic side. Conversely, salespeople usually begin on the opposite side. This is not an absolute, there are shades of gray in this area.

This phenomenon unconstructively manifests with people who spend much of their efforts on the logical side. The result is weakness in the communications area. Having great ideas, skills, and knowledge but struggling to share them constructively. A common experience is that while deep into a technical problem—troubleshooting and logic—communication skills suffer. Overall communication quality suffers when the left side of the brain is heavily engaged.

Acknowledgment of this phenomenon goes a long way toward navigating this human limitation. There is a real need to be patient with people engaged in left-brain activities. They need support in communicating. Left-brain professions often get labeled as anti-social. This is perhaps unfair. When someone is deep into the logic and mathematical space, human communication gets less bandwidth. The result is the need for social translation and compensation.

While everyone has an inherent predisposition to one side or the other, there is the possibility for growth. Left-brain-dominant individuals can work on those communication skills just as right-brain-dominant folks can work on numbers, etc. Even small, incremental improvements deliver real value to your project management efforts.

Say thank you

A secret weapon—the polite, professional follow-up. Politeness has value. Saying thank you demonstrates that you are paying attention and have empathy. A thank you also acknowledges the communication and closes the loop that the message was received. Open-ended communication in the modern work environment is a pervasive challenge. The assumption that the receiver received the message, knows about it, and realizes the content has value is not valid without a confirmation. A two-word reply of "thank you" confirms all those assumptions. This reply makes for a tighter and more effective communication environment.

Take advantage of old-fashioned politeness. Make this part of your positive communication style. Politeness can put a constructive spin on tension goals.

If you are reliably polite, people will notice when you are not. This can also be useful.

PARALLEL COMMUNICATIONS

> Let's ask a lot of people the same
> question. What can it hurt?

Someone has a question they wish to have answered quickly. They know of several people who may have the answer. Individual, identical emails are sent to each potential sources for the answer. The emails are sent within moments of each other. Multiple people receive an identical question and likely begin acting on the request. Now multiple people in the organization are now performing identical work. Once the first person answers, the request will have been satisfied. The equally valid, but more tardy responses represent wasted resources. In a selfish effort to get what they want, the originator of the request just cost the organization time and energy that can never be realized for anything of value. Now multiply this across a large organization. The cost is significant.

This *Parallel Communications* phenomenon is one of the most pernicious communication phenomena. Why? There is an ironic comedy to the activity. In the process of attempting to achieve rapid results, resources are needlessly consumed, thus preventing other activities. Those other activities are then delayed in realizing their value. It's common but, paradoxically, rarely recognized or understood. A phenomenon as rampant as it is costly.

With parallel communications, different groups communicate and engage on the same topic while being ignorant of each other's efforts. The issue is that communications are not inclusive. To avoid parallel communications, always copy relevant stakeholders on any email exchanges. Invite them to meetings. Be inclusive. Consolidate email strings into a single communications channel. Otherwise, parallel communication streams develop. Problems are shared and resolved without key stakeholders being in the know.

A variant of parallel communications is called shotgunning. This occurs when someone is looking for a single piece of information and subsequently shoots off a bunch of emails, instant messages, and calls to several key people. Usually in the hunt for a single piece of information. The leviathan-sized opportunity cost of shotgunning is poorly understood, representing a hellishly expensive consumption of resources while several people look for the same single answer.

Many individuals engaging in parallel communication and shotgunning do not realize they are doing it. Gently raise the visibility of this phenomenon. Most people will acknowledge the situation and self-correct. A select few may require more overt guidance. For the most part, those who are enlightened on this topic appreciate reducing or eliminating this phenomenon from their professional communications experience.

Run Silent, Run Deep

Silence is a powerful tool. Most people cannot stand periods of silence during a conversation. It is something that can be used for emphasis during a presentation and for persuasion when negotiating. Silence can move mountains if implemented correctly. Ask a question and go silent. Wait and wait if necessary. The answers will be forthcoming. This is another skill requiring practice. Once developed, it feels like having a superpower.

When used in combination with *Forty-Three Seconds*, silence is amazing. Deliver a polished, thought-out, forty-three-second message, and then stop and wait. The audience will respond, the silence prompting them to comment or ask questions.

The countermove to silence is silence.

There is a saying: It is nice to be first, but the money is often in being second. This is true with silence. Be quiet, take it in. Use the time to plan the next question or reply.

A variant on this is to remain silent during most of a meeting. Listen and hold off for the end. Let those who must talk, talk. At the conclusion is the opportunity to summarize the whole meeting and close. This maximizes focus on the last few minutes of the meeting. Let others be first, then be the closer by going last.

Welcome to Middleman Hell

The concept being shared here is the primacy of knowledge management in the project management environment. Absorbing, evaluating, responding, and redistributing information to support project execution.

During a job interview, the hiring manager brought up the subject of communication. The applicant shared that in a previous role much of what was done was to move information around. To be honest, others did most of the actual "work." One of the skills they would bring to this new role was expertise in being the go-between for information. Also, their experience engaging different people, vertically and laterally, both inside and outside the organization. Being in the middle of everything was a familiar role.

Project management is a communicate, organize, and execute position. To be honest, others do most of the work. Considering the array of talent and skill needed to achieve most anything worthwhile in a modern project, this makes sense. Marketing and sales know their jobs, as do engineering, quality, etc. In a project, a focal point that ties these contributors together is required. Hence, there is a project manager.

Being the focal point is not all that different from being in senior management. Project management often interacts laterally and vertically across the organization. Likened to a spider in the center of a web, managing information and communicating to deliver project success.

A project manager's primary skill is communication. A close second is analyzing information and being discriminative in its distribution. Project managers often act as a central clearinghouse for information, determining who needs to know what and when.

An often-overlooked aspect of the information dimension is awareness of what should be shared. Aligning information with contributors to keep the project executing. Processing information is not a passive activity; it is more than just taking information and putting it places like a postal worker places letters in boxes. It is important to confirm accuracy, time criticality, distribution, and confidentiality.

This management of information flow requires active engagement. An email from a senior manager may need to be rephrased and shared in a text or on a phone call. Information may need to be grouped until it reaches critical mass—or saved to satisfy a future request. A straightforward product-quality resolution may require face-to-face discussions with technicians who are finding the root cause of a problem. Or perhaps collaborating with Quality to create the document to share with the final customer.

Each of these groups will have a different focus and respond to a different language (*Speak the Language*). An array of communication skills will be needed. At some point, the conclusion dawns that communication is every bit as technical and complex as many modern technologies.

Communications gone bad

A salesperson is visiting a customer who relates a technical challenge. The salesperson replies they do not have the answer but will bring the engineer along at the next visit in two weeks. The customer's need is not immediate, and they agree to wait until the next visit.

Two weeks later, the salesperson and subject-matter-expert engineer sit down with the customer.

The customer tells them about the application, their approach, and the unproductive outcome.

The engineer looks at the customer and asks, "Why are you doing it like that? That's stupid."

This urban legend is an extreme example of communication gone bad. But there are situations, communication styles, and sometimes people delivering outcomes not all that different from this story.

Communications can secure success as well as deliver failure. Awareness of the negative communication phenomena in project management is also a skill. Effectively identifying and navigating bad communication events is equally important to developing good communication skills.

Things best left unsaid

As information is flowing through a project manager's purview, they will often be exposed to things not commonly known or distributed. This in-between status often includes awareness of technical details or sensitive internal information that would be problematic to share externally. The situation and the details of the information require a judgment call on what should be distributed. What is needed here is a sensitivity towards recognizing when something is ready to be external-facing. Internal communications detailing a quality issue, product strategy, or even just rumors and speculation must be interpreted through the "shareable information filter." In just seconds, the filter engages and delivers the conclusion "this will never be shared." The shareable information filter is similar to the CONFIDENTIAL filter. Discriminating between internal-only versus external information is a skill. The next level is protecting genuinely sensitive confidential information. Understanding these distinctions and their legal implications is important.

Compartmentalizing information should only happen if it is truly business sensitive. The suggestion here is to distribute information as broadly across the project participants as possible. Nothing is held back unless it could be interpreted as inflammatory or there are legal implications.

There are occasions where information needs to be shared, just not in writing. The only channel for this is verbal. Face-to-face or on a call. This is likely for a politically sensitive topic. **Remember: Emails are forever, as are recorded calls.**

The skill to share information broadly while still being judicious is key to successful project management. An additional benefit is others will see the care with which you handle information. This opens the possibility they will share their insights with you.

When executed well, skills around information compartmentalization, judicious distribution, and recognizing sensitive

45

information delivers increased project efficiency and overall effectiveness.

Unleash the Fury!

If frustration could be bottled and used to generate energy, project management could power the world. Misunderstandings, last-minute changes at inconvenient times, and discarding of completed work all create frustration for project managers.

In the professional work environment, frustration is a real and ongoing challenge that impacts mental health and generates strong negative emotions. Frustration is the response to unreasonable and irrational situations. If people are involved, then frustration happens.

Have you ever evaluated your frustration response?

Have you ever evaluated your frustration response?

Identifying those frustrating situations, acknowledging them, and then having a plan will help manage the situation. The evaluation process is not about ignoring frustration. The emotional response is delivering important information. Use it. The goal is to have a response that does not damage long-term relationships or add more problems. Learn to stay calm, professional, and engaged when frustrated. Work through the challenge. These situations are opportunities to demonstrate skill in resolving a difficult situation.

Frustration is often the result of poor communication. Developing communication skills will reduce the number of frustrating events to work through. Alternatively, a contributor may not be asking the right questions or has a high workload and is dealing with unreasonable requests. Assistance and guidance from an aware and skilled project manager can overcome all of these and reduce everyone's frustration.

Frustration and email (or any kind of instant messaging) are a toxic combination. Before responding while frustrated, get up and walk away. The desire to *Unleash the Fury!* will be strong. Not taking a break before responding could result in a career-limiting email. Remember, emails are forever.

Do not give in to the frustration and make sarcastic remarks, yell, or insinuate. Keeping frustrated reactions under control is one of the most challenging skills to develop.

> You cannot control the world, but you can influence the outcome by setting the tone.

People are often unaware of their word choices. They have a sense of entitlement to say what they wish or, even worse, what they feel. And they do this in any setting, personal or professional. The project manager does not enjoy this flexibility. When others are inappropriately speaking, avoid responding with anything inflammatory. It is that simple. "Simple" itself can be an inflammatory word, but in this case, it perfectly captures the absolute nature of this approach.

In addition to the never-ending effort to remain constructive and avoid the inflammatory, it will be necessary to attenuate any inflammatory communications that pass through the project manager to be shared with others.

Insinuation and gossip are verboten

Do not insinuate or gossip. It is unprofessional. Engagement can be challenging enough without needing to overcome the negativity these activities bring.

To determine if discussing a topic with a colleague is gossip, ask: Will sharing this benefit the company? If not, it is probably gossip. Or to put it another way, if what is said was recorded and played back, would the people being discussed be offended?

And there are so very many recording devices out in the world today.

Sarcasm

So much about sarcasm is cultural, situational, and tone dependent. There are those who consider sarcasm great fun and others who will take instant offense. Many cultures do not support sarcastic interaction.

> There was a Swiss company, with many French and French-Swiss colleagues. Sarcasm was not in their makeup. Perhaps it was an English-as-a-second-language thing, but anything said was interpreted literally. "Why would you say such a terrible thing?"

> While in Germany for training, a colleague shared her love of sarcasm and apologized in advance. She shared how she had to be careful because her comments, while hilarious to some people, could be taken as an insult. Thank God Germans have a sense of humor.

The point of these examples is to be cautious with sarcasm. The default should always be to keep the communication professional. You never know who is listening and how they'll interpret what you've said.

MAXIMUM TALKING, MINIMUM CONTENT: ENGAGEMENT GONE BAD

Some people just cannot stop talking.

Conversations or meetings should be like a game of tennis. One person speaks, answers a question, or makes a point. Then another person speaks, answers a question, or makes a point. The conversation goes back and forth. Everyone participates as needed and limits the discussion to the agreed topics while giving each participant the opportunity to speak.

The "how" of conducting oneself in a conversation is not universally understood. That is why this is considered a phenomenon. Everyone has been in meetings with someone who will not stop talking. Judging the level of appropriate sharing in the conversation is a sign of maturity. If one speaker is talking for more than twice as long as the other speaker(s), this phenomenon may be manifesting. As was covered in *Forty-Three Seconds,* keep to the facts and nothing but the facts. Say what needs to be said, then be silent. However, there will be meetings where a *Maximum Talking, Minimum Content* person takes over the conversation. Learn how to break in and redirect. It may be necessary to start talking over the offender and keep talking until they stop. Then redirect. Do not make it personal or bring attention to their domination of the conversation. Just redirect, doing the minimum to keep the conversation on track.

ELMO: Enough, let's move on.

If the *Maximum Talking, Minimum Content* person is a repeat offender and it is challenging to keep the conversation on course, try forming an alliance with another participant. Working together, maneuver the conversation to where it needs to be.

Over the course of a project manager's career, there will be many meetings with *Maximum Talking, Minimum Content* experiences. Learn how to identify them and guide the discussion back to something all the participants can engage in.

UNNATURAL CONVERSATION

Wish in one hand and crap in the other,
see which one fills up first (paraphrase).

The team is gathered around a conference room table. Topics are listed on a whiteboard. Perhaps a presentation is on the big screen. There is a lively discussion ongoing. People are taking turns to speak their peace. Then a topic comes up that one participant latches onto, and they keep talking about it. Expounding and elaborating, drilling down to a level of minutia far outside the scope of the meeting. And then someone else jumps on the bandwagon. A whirlwind of nostalgia, technical detail, and dreams of things for the future. *Maximum Talking, Minimum Content* manifests as a group phenomenon. Then the meeting runs out of time, ending as a gigantic waste of resources.

The above is what happens when participating in a session of *Unnatural Conversation*. Someone was bored and feeling unstimulated. When they were able to get hold of the conversation, they steered it to a tangentially related topic and then spoke at length about something they found more interesting. Others joined in. No one stopped the process, and much time was wasted.

There is a subtle difference between this phenomenon and *The Free-Association Apocalypse. Unnatural Conversation* is several participants talking ad nauseum about unrelated topics to a tiny level of detail. *The Free-Association Apocalypse* is the seemingly never-ending addition of complexity to a project without concern for practicality.

Unnatural Conversation is an unconstructive and undisciplined use of time. If the person starting it is more senior, participants might have to grin and bear it. In other situations, anticipate and strategize how to get the conversation back under control. Certain individuals are more susceptible than others to engaging in this kind of behavior. Aside from regaining control during the meeting, perhaps schedule shorter meetings where the time pressure makes *Unnatural Conversation* difficult. Making others aware of this phenomenon can also help.

A variant on *Unnatural Conversation* is what-iffing. This spectacularly unproductive application of human intellect is the exploration of unlikely, preposterous, potential outcomes from a particular course of action. The speaker, sharing in this way, is looking to end a particular path forward by loading it with questions that will take forever to answer.

Both approaches require awareness to recognize when they are happening and then to shut them down. This phenomenon is another where awareness is the most significant aspect of solving the problem. Once acknowledged, redirecting or ending the unproductive discussion is a more straightforward affair. Point out the need to return to the original discussion and that the *Unnatural Conversation* topic can be addressed offline.

CAN GOD CREATE A ROCK BIGGER THAN GOD CAN LIFT?

I am unable to answer speculative questions.

In project management, this phenomenon manifests in one of two ways. It could be either the derailing of a meeting with needless speculation or a request for something so far out of the ordinary it is difficult to respond to. This happens when either someone is trying to impress people with how smart they are or the requesting party does not understand the practical limitations of the subject being discussed. Perhaps there is a third possibility: they are just trying to see the kind of response they can get with their outrageous requests. For the purpose of this discussion, only the first two variants will be addressed.

Take the example of a meeting or conversation, often technical in nature, when the line of discussion deviates to tangentially relevant topics. There are questions or comments delivering little to no value to the meeting, or the questions require a ridiculous amount of work to answer while providing little in return. This often happens as part of *Maximum Talking, Minimum Content* or an *Unnatural Conversation* scenario but taken to a singular extreme.

This phenomenon also comes up in customer-facing engagements. Someone asks, "What if the application was upside down? At 10,000 meters above sea level, there are traces of chlorine in the air, and the operator speaks Icelandic. How would your product perform?" This scenario is so far out of ordinary operation, there is no way to answer it. To test or determine a detailed response is not worth the effort. They are essentially asking if God can create a rock bigger than God can lift.

The question serves no practical purpose. In sales-related situations, however, saying no is not an option. Just because something has never been tested does not mean it will not work. The ultimate goal is to not be held responsible for giving permission to a very non-standard application.

If there is not an answer to the question, *never make it up*. An oft-used response to such bizarre requests is to add "speculate" to the beginning of the reply. This is a popular and fitting "get out of jail free" word. Rather than saying "no" or "that is not an appropriate use of the product" (which are both negative statements), the recommended response is something like, "That has not been tested and performance is not guaranteed, but based on past performance, it is speculated the outcome could be X." It answers the question without committing to it.

Some may argue this style dodges a specific answer to the question and therefore lacks integrity and will negatively impact credibility. No, the question was hardly airtight and complete in its structure. Much is left unsaid, and the requestor asking the question is reserving the right to take a precise answer and apply it to an imprecise situation. And if the final outcome is not perfect, they WILL call you on it. With words like "speculate" and "possible but not tested," the discussion can remain engaged without delivering a commitment.

Ultimately, cases of the *Can God Create a Rock Bigger Than God Can Lift* phenomenon are a smart person scratching a mental itch or injecting extreme risk avoidance. It is likely they do not plan to implement their unlikely scenario. By "speculating" but not "guaranteeing," an answer is given without committing to anything. A response is delivered, satisfying whatever motivated the question in the first place. The "speculate" wording also pushes the liability back on the person who asked the question. Allowing the requestor's individual risk aversion to resolve the situation without need for further discussion.

Communication Complexity

The United States and Great Britain are two countries separated by a common language. – George Bernard Shaw

---

The British were possibly the most prolific explorers, colonizers, conquerors, and traders in world history. The result is English becoming the de facto global language for communication. If the English had not built an empire upon which the sun never set, it is likely the global business environment would still be trying to agree on what language everyone will use.

Professions have their own terminology and often a somewhat unique worldview. This jargon could be interpreted as a profession's own language. To better connect with these professions, learn that terminology, learn that worldview. Even if only to have a surface understanding of the profession's communication nuances. Someone in sales looks at earned revenue differently from an accountant in finance. Management focuses on top- and bottom-line performance versus sales being incentivized on the top line. Neither the top line nor the bottom line may be considered important by many engineers.

Even with agreement on a common language, there are other factors for effective communication. Achieving understanding is not so straightforward as everyone speaking English. Culture, profession, native language, nationality, and even organizational eccentricities influence how words and concepts are interpreted. If both parties are not aligned on word meanings and inference, misinterpretation occurs with increased frequency.

Adding to the complexity of profession-dependent language is the effect personalities play in this space. Different personalities find certain career choices appealing. This is not a perfect generalization, but it likely meets the 80/20 rule threshold. Likely, more than 80% of the personalities in a chosen profession will have somewhat predictable characteristics.

Working in the international arena introduces language characteristics that impact communication. Communicating with someone who thinks in a language other than the one being spoken is different than communicating with a native speaker.

Effective, Brief, Communication—Writing

Professional daily writing in the corporate environment is different than writing an essay. Most work-related written communications are short and singular in purpose. Typically, either advocating for action or soliciting/asking for information. There is little in anyone's educational experience that prepares people for writing short, concise, effective messaging. This brief, concise message skill has an almost military aspect in execution, differing from writing a longer-format white paper or document.

From a corporate standpoint, there is a significant waste reduction opportunity to be found in developing individual skills in this space. Just like needing tools to repair a car, a house or a computer, expertise in the tools used in project management—Microsoft Office®, Excel, Word, Outlook, etc. —is required. In written project management communications, words are also tools. However, the fundamental understanding of the words used and how those words are organized is also important.

A Bell Labs researcher shared his experiences with professional writing. In that environment, creating technical papers was part of the normal work routine. On one occasion, a supervisor read the researcher's latest

55

paper and delivered a blistering critique. Why did the reader have to work through the entire paper to figure out the subject? Where was the summary at the beginning?

Two outcomes came from this negative experience. The first was how the beginning of a communication is written is important to how the paper is perceived. Second, after rewriting the paper in a proper format, the researcher was made responsible for setting up and teaching an effective writing class. After all, your reward for good work is more work.

Effective writing should be considered an enterprise-wide interest. The entire organization structure from top to bottom will benefit from developing better writing skills. It is advocated here that such training not be a canned online experience. Nor a third-party trainer delivering a colorless, required training that is really nothing more than a box to be checked. Proper, effective writing training should include senior management involvement. This level of engagement lands the message: this is important.

A concept in writing a fiction novel is to share "the promise of the story," which is centered around the content of the first chapter. This is the introduction of concepts, places, and characters in chapter one. These will be woven together as the plot progresses through the rest of the book. Writing the promise is a skill. Get it wrong and nobody reads the book past page ten. Get it right, and the reader quickly becomes invested in the story. For example, go back and reread the first paragraph of chapter one of this book. Did the promise land well?

Advocate for fewer shared opinions and other tangential material.

In brief communications, having the first few sentences deliver the essence of the communication is key. That first paragraph, perhaps similar to an email subject, should be concise and descriptive. The important information in an email should be first. Professional short messaging is not an exercise in storytelling.

The purpose of brief messaging, email or instant messaging, is to exchange information or request action. Is the information clearly presented and not buried in a paragraph of text? Is the request for action clear and separate from the supporting text? Is a name associated with who's being requested to take action?

A time-saving technique with emails is to summarize forward from a string of replies. As an email string grows, aggregate pertinent information to clarify the discussion. Do not force everyone in copy to work through the previous emails. This also reduces the chances of misinterpretation and supports an effective handoff as the email progresses through its life.

Bullet-point list of effective short message structure, email, or instant message:

- Is the subject clear and relevant?
- Is the format of the body clear, concise, and organized?
- Is the important stuff first?
- Is the intent of the email, whether providing/requesting information requested or prompting action, obvious to the reader?
- Are the previous emails summarized forward into the latest email?
- Are the right people in copy?

Mastering effective, brief communication improves project execution as downstream consumers receive clear information needed to execute. This same clarity reduces errors and unconstructive ambiguity. The time savings provided by clear subjects, descriptive introduction sentences, and well-defined expectations is appreciated by all.

May the Almighty save us from the ravages of email

Emails appear to fall into three general categories:
- ➔ Something that must be read completely and acted upon
- ➔ Something to pass on. A thorough read is not needed.
- ➔ Garbage

The quality of an email impacts project execution. Below is a list of common anomalies that should be removed from practice:

Non-answer answers—The sender of the email provides an answer, often a meandering, vague, difficult to decipher reply. It does not deliver information that is actionable. All that is delivered is frustration. The response here is to ask for clarification. It is likely the sender does not conclusively know the answer but is trying to provide one. A cousin of *The Circular Firing Squad,* non-answer answers are to be avoided.

Blocks of text—The email begins with, or consists of, a monolithic, block of text.

I, I, I—People do this without knowing it. Four out of five sentences in a paragraph start with I. The writer appears to be trying to share the specifics of actions they have taken. But in written form, with so many sentences starting with I, it distracts from the message.

Another version of I, I, I is you, you, you. Watch for both I and you and remove them. The current paradigm of teamwork and collaboration drives a "we" approach. We, we, we is more easily accepted versus I, I, I or you, you, you.

Escalated forms—This is about writing for your audience. Starting an email with "Hello" is friendly and works with all audiences. Starting with "Hey" is informal and should be reserved for casual friends or maybe, close working colleagues. As the audience moves up into the senior and executive spaces, the email should be specific and direct. Skip the slang, innuendo, and vagueness.

Omission—Do not exclude information likely considered important. Having to explain why details were left out is a crime of omission. Shorting information from a communication is problematic. Especially if the email begins working its way upward in the organization and more senior management takes actions based on an incomplete picture of the situation.

Email is an efficient tool for communication. Like all tools, it must be used correctly. Everyone should put effort into their email skill set. Enhance the positive and eliminate the negative.

Editing is a real thing

The prevailing default approach to email and instant message is to type out a stream of consciousness and press send. This is a terrible practice. No one writes effective communications on complex topics on the first try, even in short communications. First write a draft then reread it. Better word choices, sentences, and paragraph structure will be revealed. Details that were missed in the first rush to write will be noticed. Developing a disciplined process takes practice. Write, read, edit, read again, final edit, and then send. Working through this approach will improve the initial email and instant message. This improvement reduces the amount of review and editing needed.

Some emails or texts are written for a critical audience. In those situations, it is reasonable to request that a colleague read the message before sending. Some people have never heard of this collaborative approach, so do not be surprised if a co-worker is skeptical at first. For those new to regularly communicating with executives, having a peer review may be prudent.

The value of editing is real, and with some practice, the realized benefits will be too obvious to skip over.

THE CIRCULAR FIRING SQUAD

Who has not sent out an email asking a question only to receive a question in return? You reply with your question clarified and re-send. The next email back is a reply about a subject tangential or adjacent to the discussion. Another party copied on the email then replies they heard another group is doing something similar, but not actually the same thing. Another participant in the communication shares this could be done better using this thing not currently part of the product, but if we ever develop it, the results would be awesome.

This phenomenon is found in those weird, never-ending email strings where no one answers anything and nothing is accomplished. Questions are answered with questions and speculation about how something *could* be accomplished. In some cases, participating members digress into topics they are more interested in.

What's happened is everyone involved is heavily tasked with little energy available for the communication in question. They are skimming the email and not engaging in what is being discussed. A rapid response is made to get this one thing done and out of their inbox, with no real mental engagement. That desire for a rapid response is another example of the need for a short and focused email. Learn to recognize the colossal time waster that is *The Circular Firing Squad* and have a strategy ready to get them under control.

Do not be a *Muddy the Water* email writer. That person, who instead of helping the effort spiral into a solution, introduces tangential concepts and work. This is similar to trying to solve everything simultaneously. It is not going to happen. There is an element of *Hooking On* in some *Muddy the water* interactions. Leveraging the situation to accomplish other things rather than zeroing in and solving this one problem.

What is the solution? Get people on the phone or face-to-face (*In Person for Maximum Effect*). This allows for a more solid engagement and delivers results faster. Sometimes you just have to talk to people.

The forms must be obeyed

Many people have the philosophy that anything in an email can be held against its creator at a future date. This is correct—emails are forever. Do not write anything in a company email that it would be regrettable to lose control or distribution of.

The ruthless approach is to minimize the word count. For example, an email that says, "Take care of this," and it has an attached spreadsheet. Nobody misses the point when reading one of these emails and none of the reader's time is wasted. However, this approach is somewhat off-putting to many. This spartan style comes across as harsh, and some readers would be better engaged with some human language included such as, "Hello John." Ending with "Best Regards" or something similar has value. Is this sophistry necessary? No, but it is easier on the eyes. In the end, email messages are intended for people, and adding some humanity to the email structure will help with the reception without cluttering the message itself.

Making the Sausage

Making the Sausage is a minimalist approach for freeing up energy. Creating a space where less polished information can be presented with the understanding that it is a draft for educational purposes only and not ready for broad distribution.

Any written creation has two elements of energy put into it. The first element is the rough original layout with all the concepts, comments, and ideas. The second element is polishing it for wider distribution. Often these are not equal levels of expended energy.

The in-process documents are the making of the sausage. They are not ready for others to review, other than as an informal reference. All the high-value elements are included, but it is not pretty. These rough drafts are efficient and conserve energy. Everything is there if you are willing to overlook the aesthetics. With rough drafts, you've accomplished 80% of the value with 20% of the energy.

It is advantageous to operate almost completely in rough materials right up until something is needed for wider distribution. This conserves energy until a final, ready-for-distribution, version is needed.

A scenario that comes up: a supervisor asks for an update on a project and wants to see some documentation. A rough draft of a document, perhaps with notes from a recent meeting, is available. These documents are sent over with a comment that they are not polished, final documents, but all the information is there.

The scenario that often plays out is after receiving this pre-polished version, the requestor comments on the rough state of what you sent. More polish would have been appropriate since the requestor shared everything with more senior managers. They were drafts! What was available was shared and declared as drafts beforehand. When sharing documents like this, it is important to put a disclaimer up front or add a watermark. *Rough Draft! Not Ready for Distribution!*

Avoiding this misuse scenario will take some practice, but maximizing documentation creation while minimizing energy consumed is a force multiplier in your project management efforts. The *Making the Sausage* approach is a way to increase your output by avoiding the finalizing/polishing time sink unless you absolutely must make those changes. Just remember to communicate this approach to prevent misunderstandings.

THE COST OF MEETINGS

How can a labor cost be a phenomenon? Because nobody acknowledges its existence. Meeting invites with everyone included are sent every second without a thought to the organizational cost. The specific phenomenon observed is that the cost of a meeting is never considered when a meeting is organized. The common approach is the more, the merrier. Meetings have direct labor costs that can be reduced and opportunity costs to manage.

Picture a mechanical odometer, the older style with the spinning cylinders, in a car. But instead of miles, the numbers represent dollars. The moment the participants arrive at the meeting, the numbers start spinning, adding up the incremental cost, minute by minute. This is the increasing dollar cost of the meeting. The higher the skill level per person, plus an increasing meeting headcount, and that cost counter's rate of increase evolves into a blur. An important goal when organizing a meeting is to minimize that cost to only what is absolutely necessary.

Consider the expense all the people in the meeting represent. Not just salaries and the cost of the room, what about the staggering opportunity cost? What could be accomplished if this particular group of people were not participating in that particular meeting?

These costs are the reason meetings should not be organized without a goal. The goal of the meeting should justify the cost. That cost is generated from the meeting's participants. Setup the meeting for good reasons and invite only those needed. Have a descriptive subject line for the meeting AND a written goal. These are the absolute minimums.

Effective meetings

> The law of inverse ninja strength—The effectiveness of a group of ninjas is inversely proportional to the number of ninjas in the group.

Just as in the movies where groups of ninjas are ineffective but individual ninjas are nigh invincible, so does the effectiveness of communication and engagement increase as the number of people involved decreases. Maximum effectiveness is achieved at one-on-one. (*In Person for Maximum Effect*) This concept applies to meetings.

Large meetings are for distributing information with little interaction. If the goal of the meeting is high interaction, then a small group will deliver better outcomes. If this is a large informational meeting, the outcome will be a common understanding. If the goal was to solicit input and assign action items, then one of the concluding actions of a meeting should be a review of assigned action items.

Effective meetings require a proactive approach that includes reasoned planning of who, why, and desired outcomes. These should be considered when the meeting is planned.

The Pre-meeting Meeting

An activity that is perhaps not understood by the casual observer is the management penchant for the pre-meeting meeting. Whenever a meeting is planned, key participants huddle beforehand to discuss strategy. It seems a needless amount of over-communicating, as the pre-meeting participants have already planned to attend a meeting on that exact subject.

The Pre-meeting Meeting is about reducing risk.

The pre-meeting meeting is about reducing risk and offers the opportunity to align on the topic(s) and resolve potential misunderstandings. Perhaps it is a good idea to double-check a question with a colleague before putting them on the spot in front of leadership. If confirmation from a colleague is expected while you are presenting, make sure they are on board with the message ahead of time. Key people need their input confirmed in advance.

The pre-meeting is an opportunity to align with your supervisor on a controversial topic before delivering the message in a setting where there is less control. If the meeting has political ramifications, there may be more than one pre-meeting meeting. This activity does increase workload, but the return on investment is reduced project friction. Particularly if developing alignment with leadership's vision is important. And if long-term success is a goal, it should be.

With the pre-meeting meeting accomplished, the actual meeting is the public confirmation of what has already been discussed and decided. The participants' comfort level will be higher, and the possibility of an unknown unexpectedly derailing the meeting will be reduced.

The Meeting Sinkhole

In Milwaukee, you can visit the Pabst mansion. The office of the founder of Pabst Brewing Company is there. In that room is only a desk. There are no chairs for anyone other than Mr. Pabst. His policy was you came in, said what needed to be said, and got out. There was no need for visitors to sit.

Project managers will organize and participate in many, many meetings. Executing a well-organized meeting that delivers constructive outcomes is a beautiful thing. Skill development in meetings benefits from the development of communication skills.

They should not just "happen." There should be a pre-planned purpose. Have a plan, and actively manage the progression of the meeting. Be proactive and mindful of what the meeting was called to accomplish. Make sure the purpose of the meeting is delivered before the end.

Meetings serve a limited number of purposes: presentation of information, solicitation of information (asking questions), assignment of tasks, and seeking consensus (making a decision). In most cases, a meeting is a combination of these basic building blocks.

> Parkinson's Law: Work expands to fill the available time

A tactic to keep everyone focused is to shorten the meeting time. Instead of one-hour meetings, try forty-five-minute meetings. Or better yet, thirty-minute meetings. A shorter duration injects tension that keeps the participants focused on the meeting and reduces the likelihood of meandering discussions. This short duration provides an excuse to bring the meeting back on topic if it starts to deviate or run long.

Conclusion: Finger on the scale

Communication skills are the foundation upon which successful project management is built. Leveraging engagement, focus, and tension requires communication.

There is an opportunity to revolutionize productivity by upgrading effective writing skills. At the very least, the situation begs for an email-writing forms manual. A solution advocated here is an in-house email quality review followed by setting up an in-house effective writing class. Probably two hours in length to include brief, fifteen-minute sessions from a senior or executive manager.

Each communication phenomenon represents the opportunity to put a finger on the scale and improve project management outcomes.

> Improving communications has little cost associated with it.

Nested inside the communication phenomenon is another phenomenon: The lack of cost in improving communication. Just a little time, some mental bandwidth, reading this book, etc. No capital equipment cost. No monthly subscription. All that is needed is the willingness to self-evaluate, improve, and accept some input from colleagues and mentors. Effective communicators and communication do not spontaneously occur. They begin with the understanding that success in all efforts is subject to expertise in writing and speaking. Communication is a skill and a craft. Accept that this is not a "simple" technical endeavor and reap the rewards.

Work on building your communication skills. The results will speak for themselves.

4

ENGAGEMENT

Engagement is connecting with others in support of project efforts and soliciting interest. It works differently depending on the person or group. People's likes, personalities, experiences, what is known and unknown, and what may need an explanation are all in play. Engagement involves listening and speaking. Planning ahead of time as well as having a canned response to specific common project engagements. Success in acknowledging these nuances leads to having foresight into the existence of related people-centric phenomena. Being able to anticipate in advance supports developing well-thought-out strategies versus responding in the moment.

> Engage people with a purpose.

Managing engagement and interest levels in different parts of the project will play a role in successful project execution. Sometimes what is needed to move the project forward is knowing the right person or knowing the "trick" to the process. Engaging with people with a purpose is the goal.

DEFINED ESCALATION: WHEN CONTRIBUTORS REFUSE TO ENGAGE

The phenomenon addressed here: Why is there never a defined path of escalation to address lack of engagement? Or the messaging of a transparent path to what the request is intended to achieve?

Everyone is busy. Many are just trying to manage their workload only to have another task required of them. In pursuit of managing their workload, a contributor may not engage constructively with the project. This may range from passive-aggressively avoiding the project manager, bringing their supervisor in for support, or leading to them directly pushing back. Sometimes this pushback is delivered in an unprofessional and inflammatory way. Usually, the person not engaging is likely reacting to workload challenges more than the project manager specifically.

> Engagement is not a given. Achieving it may be more involved than anticipated.

Working with your leadership to establish a process of escalation provides transparency and an alignment of priorities with all involved parties, which is important. Driving contributor engagement should not be adversarial or delivering some sort of "making them do it" fallacy. Engagement escalation will require a process of communication between the project manager and the contributor. When it is apparent engagement is not forthcoming, next steps are taken.

The next step in the process may be reaching out to a supervisor for guidance. There may be an opportunity for a supervisor to participate in the next meeting. Inviting the contributor's supervisor is essential at this point. This meeting may lead to clarification of priorities and certainly raises visibility of the next steps. Ultimately, this process should be professional and transparent. Avoid making it personal and scrub all communications of inflammatory language. The goal is to get the project on track while respecting the contributor's bandwidth limitations. Remember, no burning bridges. It is likely all parties involved will need to work together again.

> There is a joke about a story in the Christian Bible regarding a character named Job. After horrible tribulations were heaped upon Job and his suffering finally came to an end, God restored Job to his previous life, health, and wealth. Afterwards, Job asked the Lord, "Why, Lord? Why me?"
>
> The Lord replied, "I don't know, Job. There is just something about you that pisses me off."

There are some contributors who will not like other contributors or even the project manager. Maybe the target is new, and the offending contributor has been with the company for twenty-five years and does not view certain others as important enough to work with. Or they refuse to contribute because they see supporting the project as beneath their position in the hierarchy. Or maybe, like in the bit of humor above, there is not a proper reason, they are just a contrarian.

This is where having a pre-planned, impersonal, transparent process of escalation to elevate visibility of the lack of engagement and to seek prioritization for the collective team is needed. Figure it out ahead of time. This phenomenon will require addressing in almost every project. Have that polished, practiced *Defined escalation* procedure in hand.

THAT TIME I WAS THE RECEPTIONIST FOR A BILLION-DOLLAR COMPANY

There are contributors who are antagonistic towards each other. Perhaps a unique situation where contributors don't work well together. In some cases, it is best for everyone involved, and the success of the project, that the parties remain apart.

The opportunity here is for the project manager to deliver project engagement by working as the middleman. Contributors can be engaged on the same project without them working together directly. As odd as this sounds, this is a real phenomenon. This is when those middleman project manager skills deliver.

> An engineer worked for a company that supplied electronics for a large construction-equipment manufacturer. That equipment manufacturer was a large endeavor with annual sales over $1 billion. Every three weeks, the engineer flew out to the customers and spent the week working on-site.
>
> Different teams within the customer's organization did not communicate with certain other groups. The parties involved were quality, production, engineering, and the service group. The service and engineering groups had a particularly high level of animosity between them. The relationship was dysfunctional to the point that people were comfortable making it public that they refused to speak or work with each other.
>
> Over several months, the visiting engineer developed a supplemental role as go-between and resident expert for these different groups (*Building Bridges*). Long-term challenges were solved including putting to rest some

71

serious quality and development issues. One after another, improving his employer's credibility and positive image while delivering value to the customer.

The section title referring to being the receptionist for a billion-dollar company? The engineer's presence and contribution with this customer were so universal and constant, they enjoyed unescorted access to the entire facility. It was like being a senior manager with run of the place. The receptionist would hand out a badge on Monday, and he was good for the rest of the week.

One day, after walking into the main lobby and exchanging pleasantries with the receptionist, she requested he stay for a few minutes while she ran an errand. The message was to explain to anyone coming in the front door that the receptionist would be back in a few minutes.

For five minutes, anyone walking into that lobby was greeted by someone that was not actually employed there. The insight being shared here is that constructive engagement over time can deliver on a level not likely thought possible on day one.

BE VERY NICE TO THE RECEPTIONIST

During project management people engagements, whether it's with the receptionist or someone else, be aware they may be someone who has connections throughout the company. These connections do not show up on the organizational chart. Just because a colleague or project contributor did not climb the ladder does not mean they do not have a relationship with those who have. Especially if they have a long tenure with the organization. Gossiping or insinuation can have consequences. Many receptionists or office managers are the nexus for information and wield influential power. They have unspoken alliances best not crossed. Additionally, there are those higher up in the hierarchy who will be protective of this person.

> Just as poor behavior can have a negative impact, so too can good behavior get a nod from the right, well-connected person.

How is this a people-centric project management phenomenon? These below the surface connections are just that: out-of-sight. Yet people keep engaging with colleagues as if such connections do not exist.

Be positive

Approachability and a positive demeanor are maybe second or third on the list of beneficial characteristics after credibility and integrity. People respond positively to a positive interaction. This positivity increases the quality of project engagement. Having constructive tension driving a project is important. Being positive opens the door to contributor interest. Enthusiasm can grow from interest and a positive environment, and contributor enthusiasm will deliver the best project outcomes.

Whining and complaining to management is not a strategy for success. Leadership is not a surrogate set of parents who tolerate poor behavior. Additionally, managers have a high gain setting. Even the smallest and seemingly unimportant detail may receive an uncomfortable level of scrutiny. The more elevated a manager is in the organization, the more the level of inspection of details increases. And they do not make this sensitivity public. An inappropriate word choice on the part of someone who does not understand the rules is problematic.

Management is sensitive to people not working together. Antisocial behavior, public displays of refused collaboration, and passive-aggressive actions will be noted. Leave this unconstructive behavior to those who are comfortable being unemployed. This forms the foundation and leverage point for a *Defined Escalation* strategy. There is an expectation that everyone works together.

Cultivating a candid relationship with your immediate supervisor is a beautiful thing. Critical information can be shared whenever it is just the two of you in private. Be judicious with your supervisor's boss in meetings or conversations. Frame things in a positive way. Even if others start complaining or making negative statements, do not join in.

In interactions with management senior to your bosses' boss, a project manager should always be a ray of sunshine. *We did great things today, we are doing great things tomorrow, this will be a great year, and next year will be even better.* Do not be the one to deliver a message other than positive awesomeness to leadership above an immediate supervisor's level. Following this strategy with senior/executive management also prevents the unfortunate situation where news delivered is not in alignment with a supervisor's last update to their boss. Now the big boss has two conflicting messages. The official one from a supervisor and another one—likely poorly structured—from a whiny employee.

Good luck with that.

Respect the people

Being genuinely respectful is a skill. It is about acknowledging others' value as people. What does respect look like? It looks like not interrupting people, listening to what they are saying (*Run Silent, Run Deep*), remembering what was said, and responding in a timely manner (*Close the Loop*).

Being respectful lowers stress and builds credibility. Contributors are people, not resources or work-delivery robots. Be polite and professional. Say hello. *Say thank you.* Demonstrate having a personality.

Make working with you interesting. Don't be a jerk. If the roles were reversed, would you want to work with you? Don't self-identify as antisocial. Positive messaging is the winning play in most circumstances. Demonstrate you are a team player. This means working with *everyone*. No exceptions. Engage, communicate, and participate regardless of personality conflicts or past challenges. Never let a dislike or lack of compatibility with a person interfere with the necessary professionalism and engagement. Don't commit the unforgivable corporate sin: refusing to work with others.

Would you want to work with you?

Once upon a time, at a regional branch of an international company, someone thought it would be amusing to fill out a fake complaint about a local manager behaving inappropriately. This resulted in the HR manager visiting to investigate.

After inviting the manager to take a break offsite, the HR person gathered everyone together in a room to discuss the complaint. Apparently, there was a long-running feud between several of the participants. It had nothing to do with company operations. They just did not like each other and decided that was enough to justify neither speaking nor constructively working together. A challenging situation for management to endure, only tolerated because it did not interfere with company operations.

As everyone entered the room and selected a chair, one individual decided to sit away from the others. The HR manager asked them to join the group. They refused, preferring to sit apart.

That individual was let go not long after. The action of defiantly sitting apart had identified them as a problem.

The moral of the story: Don't air your dirty laundry or act anti-social in front of the HR manager.

Respect the people and constructively engage your colleagues, even if you are not fond of them.

Contributors understand when a project manager checks up on their efforts. What is not appreciated is, "Are you done yet? Are you done yet? Are you done yet?" (*Full Kamikaze*) Respect what the recipient perceives as reasonable and tailor update requests accordingly.

Know your audience when asking for updates

Different people have different update-request tolerances. Some should be checked in on every week. Others require a longer time frame to get some work done before a check-in. Each person is different and figuring out the respectful pause duration between check-ins is a skill developed over time (*Constructive Persistence*).

The final piece of the respect puzzle is recognition. When someone makes a contribution to the project, such as dedication, extraordinary talent, or a good job, recognize them. Bring it up in a meeting in front of leadership. If the organization has a formal recognition process, learn how it works and use it.

Long term, contributors will readily engage in future efforts with a project manager who respects them.

Sales 24/7

An undergraduate engineering education included a class titled "Quality." It had nothing to do with quality in the general sense. It was really a class about what an engineer's real-world career experience could be like. The professor had numbered rules. The first was that everyone is in sales all the time. Every meeting, every call, is selling the path forward.

The world looks at an individual through the lens of what they write, say, do, and look like. Each of those is a reference on how to persuade others. Add to these the fifth characteristic: *Credibility*. Behind education, experience, skills, and the role assigned are these five background items influencing success.

Polish these characteristics and improve the chances of persuasion. Even a minimal injection of sales skills into a project manager's approach will reduce project friction and increase contributor engagement.

SHOW ME THE MONEY!

A former Bell Labs researcher was asked by his colleagues why his projects were being funded and theirs were not. His answer: show management the financial value. Showing financial value should be presented upfront. The business value is all too often an afterthought, only represented in a spreadsheet justifying the project's expense. Instead, it should be an integral part of project discussions. This is the core of the *Show Me the Money!* phenomenon.

The management experience is driven by budgets, efficiencies, ROIs, and labor costs. They communicate in money. Approaching with a value proposition is key. If influencing management is the goal, at a minimum, some part of that discussion must include money. What is the financial benefit? The "I feel this" or "Wouldn't this be nice" approaches will fail. Management will be diplomatic in the reply you receive, but this feel-nice approach will accomplish nothing. If action from management is the goal, show them the money.

Project management is not a selfish activity

> If there was ever a role requiring servant leadership, project management is it.

Project success should not be just about you. The goal is the execution of the project and the success of the organization and your colleagues. Supporting your colleagues' and contributors' success is an important part of the project.

A forward-looking project manager does not need to cheerlead for themselves by saying, "Look at me." Your excellence will be obvious through your achievements. Instead, use the goodwill generated from delivering quality results to build up the team. Invest the political capital generated from a successful project outcome forward to future success (*Credibility*). This builds a positive, self-reinforcing team. Share your colleagues' excellence with leadership. Give credit where credit is due.

When others know being on your team (or tangential to your team) delivers a positive outcome for all involved, it benefits future projects.

THE IMMOVABLE OBJECT VERSUS THE IRRESISTIBLE FORCE

There are points in a project's development where specific aspects must be frozen in place until they have been completed. No last-minute updates or scope changes. This is often related to a window of opportunity, defined delivery date, or resource availability. The milestone must be achieved without changes. There are always project-scope pressures, small or large changes being injected for various reasons. Be mindful of the impact these changes will have on the big-picture delivery or critical-resource deployment. If there is a conflict threatening carefully laid plans, the immovable-object approach can be deployed. Engage your supervisor so they are aware of the critical situation and why making changes will impact the big picture. With that foundation in place, figuratively plant your feet and refuse to make changes. Be polite and professional. Fully disclose and explain the situation to all stakeholders.

Be prepared to repeatedly defend the need to keep project aspects frozen. Those who wish to influence project scope and make changes will be persistent. They will likely reapproach several times, often with allies in tow. They will present varied arguments for why the project should be modified.

When deploying this strategy, it is important to have thought through the "why" in detail beforehand. Is this really the right thing to do? If you truly believe the project scope cannot be changed at this time for very good reasons, then stand your ground.

There is a caveat. Be aware of who is involved when implementing the immovable object approach. A peer may understand, but someone senior may see your effort as insubordinate. Make sure your plan is approved by your supervisor before executing it in front of a senior manager.

The irresistible force is the diametric opposite of the immovable object. This is a tactic applied when a straightforward ask is not enough. In many ways, the irresistible-force approach is a form of change management. A contributor is resistant or unable to collaborate. Needed resources are being withheld. The goal is to get a yes without bullying or annoying someone to the point they no longer wish to work with you (*Constructive Persistence*). Simultaneously, the goal is to portray the ask as imperative in order to get buy-in. The irresistible force is typically deployed over several engagements. Each engagement will require a different approach. New reasons, different allies.

The immovable object approach can also be a tactic for evaluating support for an action. By providing resistance, it forces those who support the action to stand up and fight for it. This provides the opportunity to gauge and quantify support. The project manager is taking short-term hits to clarify an objective.

Deploy these strategies with care. Consider them expert-level approaches. But if you can master these, achieving the almost impossible becomes possible.

LET'S FIGURE THIS OUT BEFORE THE ADULTS GET INVOLVED

There are people who are contrarians. Those who don't work well with others or have monumental egos. Whatever their major malfunction is, they will slow or even stop project progress. They are putting their personality and conflict with others before the success of the project.

In spite of being present in every workplace, people keep picking fights for the fun of picking fights. Someone will then take it too far and prevent collaboration and progress. Yet, people keep doing this over and over. Pushing it until management is forced to intervene and make everyone play nice. *Let's Figure This Out Before the Adults Get Involved* is the definition of a people-centric project management phenomenon. It is common to almost every project and impacts project execution. Rarely planned for, an most project managers or contributors do not have the tools at the ready to resolve the situation (*Common Language, Defined Escalation*). Communication skills are core to resolving this phenomenon.

If management's expectations have been shared and contributor progress is not delivered, there will come a point when leadership will engage and inspect the situation closely. Management is not looking for opportunities to solve problems. When they must get involved and realize the problem is due to one person not working with the rest, they may become critical. People are not hired to purposefully demonstrate incompetence or an inability to work with others.

This "adults getting involved" phenomenon requires at least two people for it to occur. If the task in question could be performed by the project manager, it would already be complete, and there would be nothing to discuss. This means someone is not engaging. Make sure it is not you. The contributor may have good reasons for not engaging. As project manager, you will not.

The approach proposed to mitigate these situations is if, after all escalation efforts have failed (*Defined Escalation*), share with the team how to should work this out while stating, "Before the adults get involved." Positive collaboration is important. Advocate for the team performing as needed without management micromanaging. If, after all this effort, progress remains elusive, then this is probably the time to update your supervisor on the situation (*Management Loves Surprises!*).

Excellent communication skills are needed to address these situations. Even with acknowledgment and skills, this phenomenon can be problematic. There are contributors who will refuse to acknowledge the situation and continue to resist engaging responsibly. Thereby forcing the issue to the undesirable management-mediation outcome.

CREDIBILITY

There is the phenomenon where some project managers seem to effortlessly execute through difficult projects while others have to act as a battering ram for each step of progress.

Examination of a sales call gives insight into the impact of credibility on producing forward motion. The sales representative was seventy-two years old. The supporting engineer was much younger. The goal was to attempt to convince a tier-one automotive supplier to purchase a new product. This specific offering was something the young engineer had spent a few years developing and had a patent on. He was THE subject matter expert and delivered the initial presentation. The detailed pitch was perhaps five minutes. (not *Forty-Three Seconds* compliant)

When the engineer was done, the potential customer scowled and said, "I don't know if this is something we are interested in."

It happens. Sales take work, and time, and often a number of spaced-out attempts to land the message.

The older salesman jumped in. What he said was almost verbatim what had just been shared.

The customer nodded his head: "You know, that seems a good approach."

And just like that, the customer was ready to move forward.

The young engineer was confused. His explanation had been virtually the same. The salesman had copied him. Why was the customer now ready to consider the product?

Years passed before the engineer began to understand what had just happened. Let's call it the "grey hair force multiplier": age and experience perceived as credibility that in turn influenced the outcome. Some might complain about how this is unfair and strangely discriminatory. It likely is. This falls into a "Don't blame the player, blame the game" situation. Everyone is looking to rely on the lowest risk information available, and experience delivers this. Experience and age are often associated. This is a logical outcome, even if frustrating for those on the lesser age and experience side.

Use this knowledge to your advantage. Leverage an experienced subject matter expert for credibility (*Allies*) and respect the level of influence someone experienced can bring to the effort. Difficult and time-consuming to establish, credibility makes the difference between effortless, high-efficiency project execution and the death march experienced by those less trusted. Credibility makes everything so much easier. From credibility flows trust. Trust delivers that honest collaboration needed to move quickly and efficiently. Credibility and trust are secrets to reducing friction in project execution.

Where does credibility come from? Integrity and experience combined with predictability in personality and action. It is not just a function of following rules as written. If sociopathic behavior is demonstrated—or actions that foster the perception someone is not a good-faith partner—credibility is destroyed. This is about more than being technically correct or demonstrating skill in executing an organized project. Does a project manager finish what they start? Is what is promised also what is delivered? Are the political ramifications of the project taken into account? Is the agreed-upon schedule being honored? Most importantly, when things go wrong—and they will—are colleagues and leadership receiving a timely heads-up and request for assistance before the situation turns into a tragedy? If the project manager is an unknown, getting buy-in from contributors will be more challenging. A lack of familiarity is also a lack of credibility. This makes it especially difficult for new hires thrown into the project management role. They lack the history to establish credibility.

Communication and credibility work together. Several communication-related phenomena impact credibility (*Never Make It Up, Close the loop, Deliver or notify, Perform Due Diligence*). The skills addressing the related phenomena help build credibility.

Credibility should be jealously guarded. Once lost, it is a longer path to restore than the original effort was to establish it. Establishment, improvement, and maintenance of credibility are required to develop an effective project management brand.

Integrity

Demonstrating integrity in your activities can only help you in managing a project and in your relations with your colleagues and leadership.

A story given in reply to the interview question, "Give an example of a time where you had to make a decision demonstrating integrity."

The example shared was about a factory mechanic. The kind with the associated roll-away toolbox and tool belt. It was a good job with many opportunities to learn and accomplish.

The mechanic's supervisor was in his fifties, experienced, and knowledgeable. For any skilled task performed in a factory, he was more than proficient. He was also a good teacher and would take the time to get his people to their achievable limits.

The supervisor was also a Vietnam combat veteran. Two Purple Hearts, one for being shot, the other for shrapnel in a mortar attack that scarred his face for life. He was a stable and reasonable boss, but if you crossed him, God help you. Life had been rough on him, and he was mean.

Junkyard-dog mean. And he had killed people (in Vietnam, at least).

Here is the part where integrity was tested.

After almost a year in the job, the supervisor called the mechanic out into the parking lot. The general manager was transferring to a new role, and his leased vehicle needed to be returned. The supervisor wanted the mechanic to pop open the dash and try to roll back the odometer.

The mechanic declined because turning back the odometer is illegal.

Most people would say that refusing the supervisor's request was not difficult. Really? The guy being refused does all the company terminations, has been shot before, and has killed human beings. Honestly, it makes one wonder if the mechanic was in his right mind for saying no.

The supervisor did not fire the mechanic and was okay with him saying no. Some respect might even have been earned that day.

Most employers have integrity training telling you to do the right thing, blah blah blah. But when integrity is really needed, it will be sorely tested. If you can pull off integrity without triggering a bad outcome, you may have a bright future ahead.

Most people will not have such severe integrity tests. The challenge appears to be in recognizing when situations requiring good judgment occur. In the rush to find the most efficient path to delivering some aspect of the project, you may cross a line without knowing it.

One last comment on integrity. During the drive to establish and maintain it, don't become a crusader looking for problems to weigh in on. Stick to your swim lane and focus on assigned work. The world is full of shady situations; nothing constructive will be accomplished looking for problems.

PERCEPTION IS REALITY

There are videos of people wearing virtual reality goggles and reacting as if what they see is real. Screaming uncontrollably and running into walls to escape video game monsters. Their perception is their reality.

Project management is about the practical accomplishment of tasks, not bringing the light of universal truth to the world. Do not start with telling people their perception is wrong or not real. Develop perception sensitivity and the communications filter needed to constructively engage this phenomenon.

The most visible perception a project manager will need to manage is that of project progress. The sensation of forward movement in a project is important. It inspires confidence in management and contributors. There is a requirement for others involved with the project to know work is being accomplished, and the project is realizing its value. To improve this perception, it is sometimes necessary to complete shorter aspects of a project to deliver that needed sense of forward motion. If too much time goes by with nothing perceived as happening, there will be questions.

Managing perception is a skill. Respect others' perceptions to maintain constructive relationships, and communicate project progress to provide that needed sense of accomplishment.

Never make it up

During customer visits, the sales manager does most of the talking. Then, at some point in the sales meeting, one of the customer's experts would turn to the engineer that the salesperson brought along and ask a series of questions. The person(s) asking the question(s) are typically twenty-five-year-plus subject-matter-expert veterans with hardcore experience in their field. They don't ask questions like what color the product is. Their questions are rocket scientist–challenge level. For the engineer to keep their job, the expectation is for them to answer 90% of the questions when they are asked. For the other 10%, they could beg for time to gather more information.

This is a high-pressure situation. The sales manager watches to make sure a customer relationship years in the making is not negatively impacted. The customer's technical experts need correct answers, and they will know the difference. The engineer must deliver now and deliver real value.

High-pressure, deliver-now situations abound in project management. Having a ready-to-go, calmly delivered strategy is a necessity. The goal is to avoid panicking contributors or leadership. They are semi-confrontational gotcha situations where questions are asked with the expectation of an immediate, complete, and accurate response. There will be an urge to give a reply now, even if what is said is made up. Making up an answer for convenience or to end a pressure situation is the same as telling a lie. Nothing crashes credibility like being caught saying something misleading. Getting back lost credibility is almost impossible. Something earned from years of effort can be lost in minutes.

Learn to recognize these situations as they occur. Then stay calm and execute that practiced, polished response. Have a plan, and never make things up.

Close the Loop: your follow-up game

There was an executive manager who had the best follow-up game. No matter your role in the company, from top to bottom, if asked a question, he would get you the answer.

Sometime within the next two weeks, the answer would be delivered by phone or show up in an email, or in some cases, someone else would provide the answer after the question was passed to them. This follow-up reliability reduced everyone's stress.

Always follow up. This may require a written follow-up list to keep track. There are times when two weeks have gone by and when the follow-up is delivered, there is surprise in the voice of the recipient. They thought they had been forgotten, and now they will never forget who took care of them.

The follow-up concept also applies to closing the loop on communications. Do not assume the other parties "got it." Be explicit. "I apologize for double-checking on what is probably commonly understood, but is xx planned?" In today's world of communication overload, details can be overlooked, or the messaging was poor, and a follow-up delivers needed alignment.

From a credibility standpoint, the best follow-up is in-person (*In Person for Maximum Effect*), with by phone being second. Email is the lowest quality of follow-up, but in many cases, a concise, well-structured email is sufficient. For those tough follow-ups, call or meet in person. This builds credibility by showing you are a good-faith partner who cares enough to deliver the message verbally.

Solid follow-up execution builds credibility and drives project success.

A final insight on determining if the loop was closed: just ask, "Did I answer your question?"

Attitude is everything

Project management can be a never-ending source of frustration. Perhaps one thing to keep in mind is that any project of value will be challenging. **If this were easy, everyone would be doing it.**

There are several attitude-related topics to share. Insinuation is forbidden and is poison to an organization. If the facts are not in evidence, never insinuate. We all know who the dishonest, backstabbing slackers are. Do not gossip about it. Avoid speaking negatively about colleagues.

Deliver or notify

Delays happen. Sometimes they happen often and for reasons beyond the project manager's control. It's a difficult position to manage when there is a strong demand for what you are managing, but you can only deliver delay messages instead of the final deliverables. Regardless, keep everyone involved updated. Make the call—voice is better; in person is best (*In Person for Maximum Effect, Close the Loop*). Keep the stakeholders informed. A few of them may grumble, but in the end, regular updates only increase your credibility.

If someone is expecting a reply and there is a delay while waiting for the information to pass along, let them know it is being worked on. Also acknowledge all update requests regarding delays in work or delivery. Staying connected demonstrates competence. Over time, this will turn into a sixth sense, a little voice telling you an update is due (or past due). You have mastered this skill when you deliver an update and they say, "I was just about to call you about this."

YOUR CHOCOLATE IS IN MY PEANUT BUTTER, MY PEANUT BUTTER IS IN YOUR CHOCOLATE: THE EQUAL AUTHORITY CONUNDRUM

A customer's new product design was not performing to specification. Development was falling behind, and visibility had been escalated. The supplier of a key component was identified as the source of poor performance. The sales manager supporting this customer demanded engineering support to prevent the situation from turning into a debacle.

This prompted a customer visit from the sales manager and engineer. Their arrival was greeted by THE internal subject matter experts in the design of the customer's product. Brilliant and representing decades of experience, the customer's engineering team was made up of global leaders in their field. They had thoroughly investigated and documented the problem and presented this information for review.

The shared documentation demonstrated that the problem was real. The customer's application was not performing properly. It also quickly became evident the supplier's components' basic design and physics could not be the source of the problem. How was this conclusion reached? Because the engineer was the subject-matter expert for the component and knew his craft.

For many, this would be the end of the engagement. Inform the customer the problem is not caused by the component and get an early lunch.

However, that would be a rookie mistake. Figuring out the problem did not originate with the manufacturer's component is the low-engagement answer. The opportunity here is to help figure out what fundamentally went wrong.

After figuring out the supplier was off the hook, the engineer shared steps to take to isolate the issue. The observation shared: The performance issue is firmware, not hardware.

A week later, confirmation came that it had indeed been a firmware math error.

The complete story that came out after the fact is that the customer had a hardware development team and a firmware development team. Both competent and capable. But when something did not function correctly, each team started blaming the other. Without a mechanism to break the deadlock, this could go on forever, one side claiming the other's chocolate is in their peanut butter, the other side saying, no, your peanut butter is in our chocolate. The teams had equal authority, and the problem created a deadlock condition.

How do you resolve this when teams point at each other as the source of the problem? And how do you do it quickly before damage to relationships occurs? Or even worse, management begins inserting themselves into the situation (*Let's Figure This Out Before the Adults Get Involved*).

The customer's solution was to bring in a competent third party (the supplier) and make it their problem. The supplier then acts as a semi-neutral arbiter, providing suggestions to break the deadlock.

These equal authority conditions can be difficult to resolve and may be the basis for the consulting industry. Bring in a respected third-party consultant, supplier, or subject matter expert and task them with resolving the situation.

This works because the third party bring several of the following to deliver resolution:

- They know people.
- They know things.
- They can do things.
- They have done things.
- They can assist in resolving peer-level conflict.
- The money paid to them is leverage to force action.
- They can be a willing or unwilling scapegoats.

Project contributors who are peer-level may experience a deadlock situation. Resolution may require a third party. This could be a subject matter expert, the project manager, management, or, as in the example, an external resource.

Be prepared for the *Your Chocolate Is in My Peanut Butter, My Peanut Butter Is in Your Chocolate* situations. A polished resolution delivery will minimize emotionalism. This is an opportunity to lead through the challenge by putting together the right team to deliver resolution.

Thank God Someone Knows What They Are Doing

This section is about getting the most out of people whose specialties are critical to project success.

Six degrees of separation—There is a theory that everyone is only separated from anyone else on the planet by no more than six people in succession. Finding subject matter experts follows a similar process. Fortunately, in most organizations, it will only take one or two people to find who is needed. This is shared as much for comfort as practical knowledge.

> You are likely closer to a needed expert than expected.

When possible, never rely on a single source of information; get multiple sources—sometimes even the most talented expert gets it wrong. There is nothing wrong with double-checking. Even more so if critical project elements will depend on the information shared.

Peer review of project elements—because you make mistakes and people make mistakes. Develop your peer review network. Trusted colleagues who will provide a review and quality feedback.

Shaking the tree—soliciting a reply using semi-inflammatory messaging. Sometimes the support received is lackluster. There may be an opportunity to increase tension with a poorly worded email questioning what has been shared. This will get someone's attention and therefore their focus. The goal here is to get good information, not make people angry. Be careful with the wording and apologize after for your misinterpretation. This is a devious use of *Asking Good Questions*.

> **Collaboration is required: share and grow. You are a small person if helping others gives you fear.**

There are people who don't want to share out of fear that others will now know everything they know. For instance, writing a book on project management. Has the author given away his value? Someone can just read this book and replace them. Such an approach lacks confidence and is a red flag.

Am I the author, in giving all this information away, giving away everything I know? Hardly, what is written here is only the beginning.

There is a story that is perhaps an urban myth. This was back in the 1970s. A company acquires a large mainframe computer—the kind so massive it takes up the space of a modern server room. This wonder of technology makes the company money. Real money. Executive-level-visibility money.

One day, the computer stops working. Company technicians and engineers work for a week straight without success. An engineer from the mainframe manufacturer is brought in. By the end of the second week, things are getting tense. Management bonuses are in danger, and the CEO is now personally involved.

The mainframe manufacturer's engineer pulls aside one of the company engineers to share a possible path to resolution. There is this guy who just retired who is good at fixing these things. He might be worth bringing in. This bit of information works its way up to the CEO. The nod to proceed is given.

The retired engineer agrees to consult and is flown in. Arriving on-site, he takes stock of the situation, asks some questions, and flips some switches. Then he starts opening the panels containing the computer, its peripherals, and all the wiring. After looking around inside for a few minutes, he asks for a screwdriver. Leaning back in, he tightens something. After closing the panels and a short trip back to the main control panel, he flips a switch.

The computer rumbles to life. Revenue can flow again. Consultant's total time on-site: forty-five minutes.

An elated CEO tells the consultant, "Submit your bill, and it will be paid immediately."

A few days later, the bill arrives and is brought to the CEO for approval. It has a single line item: a charge for $1,000. This is a lot of money in the 1970s for less than an hour of work. Itemization of the bill was requested. The consultant re-submits the bill: "$1 for screwing loose screw, $999 for knowing which screw to turn."

The bill was paid.

An important detail often left out of instruction in project management: expertise. Identifying the need for and engagement of subject-matter experts.

There are technical subjects and processes that present themselves when a project is being considered AND during project execution. These aspects require specific expertise not in the project manager's skill set.

Engaging subject-matter experts as a project contributor or for ad hoc input is a project management activity that can involve several phenomenon (*Asking Good Questions, Now Can You Explain It?, In Person for Maximum Effect, Say Thank You, Speak the Language, Credibility, Allies, Be Positive, Liability the Project Killer, Left Brain Versus Right Brain, Constructive Persistence, Respect the People, Smart People Think Complicated Is Fun*).

> Develop your subject-matter expert
> engagement skills.

Develop your subject-matter-expert engagement skills. Collaboration with experts is part of the project management experience. Awareness and polished communication skills are key to delivering success.

SMART PEOPLE THINK COMPLICATED IS FUN

The only thing worse than managing a room full of incompetent people lacking the needed competence is managing a room full of competent, intelligent people. Complicated approaches are easy for bright, talented people. Stand on your left foot, say supercalifragilisticexpialidocious while patting the top of your head with your right hand . . . no problem. Gaps in explanations where it is assumed the listener knows the "simple" stuff are common.

The smart people are not being malicious. For them, this really is easy. And maybe even a little fun. They enjoy working through all the obscure and inconveniently located steps in a process. After all, what is the point of having smarts without exploring their limits? Why not share the gift of intelligence with others?

For those who are not "in the know," these interactions are frustrating. The smart people are not trying to make things difficult. Honestly, they are just doing things the best way they know how and having a good time doing it. They genuinely do not understand the complexity is not well received by others.

Engaging the *Smart People Think Complicated Is Fun* phenomenon takes patience (*Constructive Persistence*) and a lot of *Speak the Language* to work through. When these smart people share information, write things down, because what is being shared may follow no rational pattern if you are not "in the know." Keep them talking. Listen carefully. In casual conversation, smart people say valuable things. Smart people associate "important" differently. Their assignment of value to information will likely be different from yours or others. This makes it difficult to just ask for that important stuff (*Asking Good Questions*).

Hugging the cactus: change management

Change management is not just another corporate slogan. It is very real with the need for a strategy. People don't like change. An effective project manager will need skills in presenting change and guiding people through the acceptance process.

The struggle is real.

Anticipating how something new will be received is as important as the delivery of the new thing. Sometimes the value of the change is explicit and positive. Project managers should take the time to shout that increased value from the rooftops. Change with complex technical underpinnings is possibly worse than bad change. Complex and technical are not fun for everyone, and abstract change is appreciated even less than the regular kind. Delivering in this space will require *Speak the Language* and *Now Can You Explain It?* skills.

> Projects change, and projects introduce change.

Then there is bad change. The most project-related bad change is a delivery date slipping. There is no joy in managing the negativity of delays and the change in expectations that comes with it. For situations like that, it is time to hug the cactus. Don't overly complicate the message, but show competency and planning for keeping the project on track. Saying, "I don't know," or shrugging your shoulders when asked about the delay is not the best path forward. Instead, look for any advantage to be gained. "This delay allows alignment with this other effort," for example. Whatever is said must be truthful (*Never Make It Up*). Change management is easier when integrity and credibility are part of the process.

A young technician is disagreeing with a senior manager. Like with many young and technically focused people, the communication is less than constructive. They are disagreeing on a change required by the manager. The technician says, "You are making me do this." The manager shakes her head, saying, "I cannot make you do anything. The only actions I can take are to sign your paycheck and call the sheriff to have you removed from the building. Everything you do here is voluntary on your part."

The point of the story is that in the workplace, nobody "makes" anybody do anything. There are levels of coercion possible through disciplinary action and threatened termination. These are explicit when

HR is involved and implicit when a more senior person directs an action. This is how hierarchy works. None of those approaches are an option for most project managers. That leaves a mere mortal project manager with influence and change management skills to motivate action. How to convince others to accept change? Or even better, support it? This is where those developed communication skills are going to pay off. Relying exclusively on the merits of your proposed change opportunity may be successful with more-engaged project contributors (those who see the value in spite of clumsy communication attempts). Unfortunately, hoping a good idea shines through a poor execution of communication is not a reliable strategy.

The path: Acknowledge you cannot make people do things. Understand you have limited authority to push change. Forego bullying as an option. Stop hoping the good idea is sufficient motivation on its own. Look to communication skill development and strategize your change efforts.

All this change-management communication takes time. What if there is no time to work through the change-management process? Perhaps there is an immediate need, and the contributor must act now. If time is of the essence, authority is needed to prompt immediate action (*Defined Escalation*).

Organizations have their own level of change tolerance versus what each individual is comfortable with. Just because the change seems like a good idea to you does not necessarily mirror what the organization supports. Organizations also do not respond well to push or pull from individuals. The goal should be to align your efforts with what the overall organization is comfortable with. Build a team consensus. Perhaps over time you may be able to shift the culture, but a short-term, glaring difference will only bring negative attention.

Mission impossible

Sometimes there is a need to find information or a person, but you don't know who they are yet.

This story takes place in Germany on a US Army post. A member of the Army Reserve with the military occupational specialty of radio repair. His first day was an interesting training initiation ritual. The new arrival is told to go get some RF grease. Then they are given a destination on post to acquire said RF grease.

Once they get to that location, they find out that location is out of RF grease, but it is possible this other location may have some. The next destination tells him they are also out of grease, and on it goes until, by the end of the day, the newly arrived soldier has toured the post and now has an understanding of where everything is.

What is RF grease? There is no such thing, just a goal for the ignorant newbie to chase after.

There are times when project managers cannot find a needed contributor or answer. Information sources available, reaching out to colleagues, even leadership, fail to deliver. The project manager's professional Venn diagram does not have a solution inside the circle. More is needed. It is difficult to find a subject-matter expert for an answer without knowing upfront who to find. Situations like this are perhaps similar to sales cold-calling.

Is there a need to bump into someone who might be able to point you in the right direction? Perhaps a meeting you must invite yourself to? You are likely to be engaging a string of people you have never spoken to before. Each of those interactions must be positive while asking for information and encouraging the sharing of the next step in the search.

Perhaps you do not even have a single colleague to start with. Time to look through the company directory and reach out. Yes, contact people you have never spoken to before. This *Building Bridges* opportunity will be an expert-level demonstration of communication skills. You'll need smooth, positive communication skills combined with sensitivity to the situation and the need to not burden the person you are randomly reaching out to. You are not there to task them with a request for work effort. Only to learn from their skilled position.

> Have you ever considered how others experience meeting you for the first time?

How can this possibly work? As long as you are polite, interesting, and do not wear out your welcome (*Forty-Three Seconds*), your unexpected reaching out breaks up the day for whoever you are speaking to. It can be fun for them if you do it right.

Contacting people without an introduction through others is not for the faint of heart. Work on this in small steps. Mentoring benefits this skill. Developing this solo might be a bit much.

Should you master this skill, your project management capabilities will have truly grown.

Conclusion: Engaging engagement

The subjects covered in this chapter build on the foundations of the prior chapters. Communication, people-centric project management phenomena, and communications skills are needed to effectively deliver engagement. Engagement is part of the process to deliver and maintain tension and focus. A good reference for improved engagement is a book by Robert I. Sutton, *The No Asshole Rule. Credibility* and *Integrity* act as lubricant in reducing project friction. They require focus to build over time.

There is a military concept that you go to war with the army you have, not the one you want. This is true in project management. The tools, your skills, and the contributors available at the beginning of the project are all there is. Success will come from leveraging every opportunity the current situation supports. Perhaps after this project is complete, or even during, opportunities will arise to improve on the available capabilities. Take advantage if this option presents itself. Until then, learn what is realistically available and plan accordingly.

5

INTERNATIONAL PHENOMENA

Project management is often an international endeavor and while English is the commonly accepted international business language, many of the people interacted with will not be native speakers. If English is not someone's first language, there are subtleties to be aware of. An example of this is how languages other than English are organized differently.

It is almost comical how the differences in language, culture, and life experience can be almost insurmountable in some ways but in other ways are similar, which indicates a singular point of understanding. Project management is one of those singularities.

Today, even small companies have international interactions. Projects involve participants in other countries for whom English is a second language. English as a second language (ESL) adds variables to the communication equation, such as organization of sentences and word choices. Learn how to exclude slang from professional speaking and writing. Speak slowly and enunciate clearly. Emails must be uniformly structured. Project participants from outside the USA for whom ESL applies should not be picking through massive paragraphs or poorly structured explanations. **If you cannot organize an email, how can you be expected to organize a project?**

An American customer purchased a product from a European company, but the product was manufactured in Asia. The players: American customer, American sales manager, European management, and two Asian manufacturing sites in two different countries with an antagonistic history toward each other. A product update was required. The East Coast sales manager was on a rampage demanding instant results. For cultural reasons, the Asian participants refused to communicate with each other. European management was concerned about the potential loss of business.

Due to the geographical situation, success in this situation can only be delivered through communication. The situation would make a business case supporting traveling to meet colleagues globally.

Here was the solution: the go-between for the antagonistic Asian colleagues acted as the communications hub (*Welcome to Middleman Hell*). All information was filtered through the one point of contact with which all parties were willing to engage with (*Credibility*). A careful scrubbing of any reference to the other involved parties was required. Strategically crafted emails and properly timed phone calls (*Asking Good Questions, Now Can You Explain It?*) kept everyone talking and delivering regular updates. In the background it was necessary to talk the sales manager down from initiating corporate Armageddon. There was nothing glamorous or fun about it, just straightforward engagement and communications.

Perhaps there is a phenomenon nestled here inside another phenomenon. When meeting someone in the international space, there is often a brief exchange of information. This initial short conversation is an acknowledgment of the geographical, national, and cultural differences. This is acknowledging that everyone has different life experiences, time zone differences, or different holidays. It is important to build a relationship with international colleagues, and this type of exchange helps. Being prepared ahead of time to engage in this type of discussion is prudent. Constructive acknowledgment of cultural differences early in your international communication efforts is a technique for quickly establishing a collaborative relationship.

Here is an example of a story of cultural differences to help build that bridge to the human side:

> An immigrant from Wales, not long after arriving in late 1960s Wisconsin began dating a local woman. An invitation for dinner at her father's home was extended. A proper, educated gentleman, he dressed in a London-made tailored suit and presented himself at the door.
>
> The woman's brother answered the door dressed in a t-shirt and jeans. His father was sitting at the kitchen table, dressed the same.
>
> The family assembled for dinner. The fall season had just begun, and the Wisconsin staple of sweet corn on the cob was served. A platter of steaming yellow corn. Which everyone eats using their hands.
>
> The traveler from afar watched all of this in horror. Who are these savages? In Wales, corn on the cob is what you feed pigs. You also do not eat with your hands.
>
> They have been married now for over 50 years.

The telling of this story of cultural differences resonates with those who regularly engage colleagues all over the world. Sharing of similar stories early in the professional relationship develops the mutual understanding of the awareness of cultural differences. The self-deprecating nature of the story also delivers the message that the teller is not ethnocentric. This story prevents misunderstandings from ever occurring.

Depending on nationality or culture, social interactions work differently from in the United States. Risk tolerance, hierarchy, communication etiquette (politeness), and education rigor are examples of where a misalignment of understanding can deliver unexpected outcomes. Risk tolerance can be low to virtually nonexistent in some cultures and nationalities. If something is not clearly written down and official, it will not happen. The low risk tolerance of international colleagues is an eternal source of frustration for Americans. The concept of operating "outside the box" or "just make it work" is a non-starter for most of the world. Also, hierarchy is crucial for most everyone outside the U.S. Again, Americans do not understand this. Americans are remarkably ignorant of formality. This is a broad generalization, but when traveling internationally, it is striking how many interactions follow a set of rules commonly known and practiced by the locals.

Politeness is required for many cultures. A "thank you" goes a long way. The rude American stereotype is justified. It is a real thing to find Americans permanently banned from any communication with colleagues in certain nations. In Europe, workdays and meetings begin with a greeting to all of your colleagues. For Americans, that is a lot of touching and interaction. The biggest in-person culture shock moment for many involves personal space. As an American, the first time European and Asian colleagues move in close while talking takes getting used to. There is an element of humor watching the new American employees experiencing this for the first time. The American steps back for more comfortable personal space. The European colleague steps forward into a space they are comfortable with. The American is literally being chased around the room.

It is problematic to approach international communications from the simplistic viewpoint that if both parties speak English, everyone will understand each other. There is a complexity to international communications that requires acknowledgment and skill development to be successful.

But it is not the same English

An engineer from France is in the USA for a week of joint sales calls. After meeting his American colleague at an east coast airport, he specifies the navigation device in the rental car be set to the French language.

While traveling down the highway, the GPS says something in French. The French colleague then glances at the American and asks, "Is this the exit?"

The American shrugs his shoulders. Maybe? Who knows? He doesn't speak French.

Having a common language is important.

Americans speak American English. The rest of the world speaks British English. There are exceptions, but these differences can lead to misunderstandings.

An American colleague was frustrated while working with an eastern European colleague who interacted with a southern European supplier. The American could not understand what they were saying even though it was all in English words. Sentence structure and word emphasis were different for each group.

To clarify communications, use basic wording, simplify sentence structure, and keep word counts to a minimum. Use words common to international English. These words are found in your international colleagues' communications. Through observation and practice, a common style emerges that is universally understood. Arriving at a common understanding requires a sophisticated approach to the situation that is delivered in an uncomplicated way.

AMERICAN IRREVERENCE IS USEFUL

Americans... you can teach them nothing.

There are opportunities in the international environment when American impertinence, high risk tolerance, willingness to think outside the box, and obliviousness to hierarchy are useful. There may be questions that need asking or people to be included, and hierarchical cultural complexities obstruct the path forward. Your international colleagues will think, "Thank God the Americans are here. They will talk to anyone, regardless of position." Americans are just that way. It is almost impossible for most Americans to comprehend the hierarchy found in other countries. This is not a criticism. Instead, this is an advocacy to appreciate the advantages of being provincial. Involving an American who can constructively engage different parties and resolve project challenges can inject efficiency into situations where nationality and cultural impacts on project execution are a challenge.

Word to the wise here: This is not a license to be stupid. Be respectful of your colleagues and sensitive to pushing too hard. A developed skill for politeness is required. If you do not understand what was just shared in this section, then you are not ready for this approach.

Traveling through time

An employer is organizing training. As a global organization, there are participants in Europe, Asia, and North America. Many people are expected to participate from Europe and Asia. Only one person from North America is participating.

The time difference between those three geographical locations is distributed in such a way that common meetings cannot be conducted during the normal hours of a working day. Someone is going to be having a meeting in the middle of the night. In this specific case, the American is going to the office at two in the morning.

These time differences play out in the project management environment. Emailing an update to a colleague in Asia just after lunch in North America will not be read by the intended recipient for half a day or more. Any expected actions as a result will take even longer. Even after the contents of the email are addressed, the reply will experience another delay on its return to the North American side.

This adds a propagation delay to communication and the taking of actions. These are important considerations when timelines and deliveries need to follow the critical path.

Conclusion—It is not as easy as it looks

International communications have characteristics that require awareness and mastery. Differences in language, culture, and, strangely enough, time must be considered. ESL will increase project execution friction without familiarization with the subtleties introduced by native language and culture. Monitor your own communications in order to attenuate your native language's lesser-known characteristics derailing your project efforts. Maintaining a tight timeline in the global environment requires consideration of time differences.

6

HOW HUMAN RESOURCE STRATEGIES IMPACT PROJECT MANAGEMENT

N-1, the Matrix, and Project Management

In the corporate environment, so much of the project management experience is tied into these two concepts: N-1 and the matrix organization. How these philosophies impact project execution is not commonly understood. Everyone is left to "figure it out." Hence, this is another one of the strange déjà vu experiences of project management.

Despite the matrix organization having been implemented decades ago, it seems many still operate in a hierarchical mindset. People tell people what to do. Like parents telling a child how to behave. A workplace hierarchy does function differently than a home hierarchy. But from that basic start develops the professional hierarchy.

Unfortunately, professional hierarchical proficiency does not prepare anyone for the N-1 and matrix experience. A structured hierarchical worldview is misleading to those who have not been clued in on what the matrix is and its practical implications. There is some unlearning to do before the complexity, flexibility, and demands of navigating the matrix can be understood.

Each phenomenon presented previously, and the potential tools for those situations, stand on their own. But when combined and applied in the N-1 or matrix environment, additional characteristics become apparent. A portfolio of skills addressing project management phenomena improves project execution in the N-1/matrix space.

THE SELF-ORGANIZING FALLACY

A maintenance team was in crisis. Everyone's workweek was at, or exceeding, sixty hours, but they were unable to keep up. The plant engineer took over managing the team and determined the team suffered from a lack of organization. Work assignments were not planned. Expertise was misapplied or nonexistent. Individuals often worked on what they liked, not what was critical to the organization.

The team was, for the most part, made up of hardworking people with good intentions. But they did not know how to organize and execute. Actions were taken to focus the team. Three shifts were consolidated to one and a half. Tasks were assigned and inspected. Expertise was introduced, and distractions were eliminated.

Six months later the team had been reduced to five people, each working forty-five hours a week, and plant uptime had improved dramatically. The labor savings more than paid for the new plant engineer's salary. Organization delivered value to the employer on an impressive scale.

Organic self-organization is a fallacy.

The key takeaway from that experience: People do not organically organize. They need guidance and leadership. This conflicts with a commonly held belief that people in small groups self-organize. No, they do not. The propaganda sets expectations that confuse people when teams are created and given instructions to execute. The participants think they will gel organically, and natural self-organization will take over. This creates frustrations when the team dynamics do not meet expectations. There are natural leaders who intuitively organize people. And there are those who have worked with such a leader and learned from them how it is done. The remaining balance of humanity has no idea how to properly organize, collaborate, and work together as a team. Taking a group of people, calling them a team, and telling them to organize and make things happen is problematic. And that's regardless of their education, skill, or individual intellect. A well-organized and executing team is a beautiful thing, and they rarely organically occur.

There is a trick to getting water out of a bottle faster. First, move the bottle in a circular fashion to get it swirling. The results are startling. The water exits the bottle so much quicker than pouring it straight out.

There are people who know these "tricks." Learn how to find the project management versions. Most project managers are not concerned with getting water out of bottles. But they are concerned with improving project execution. Getting contributors organized and the resources in the right place can deliver an outcome that will feel similar to watching the swirling water exiting that bottle.

Working effectively as a team is a discipline and learned skill. Experience and maturity improve the collaborative experience. Exposure to a capable and competent leader will help develop skills in this area. Associate with these people whenever possible. Make yourself useful to them and learn those leadership skills.

Your goal: Find an experienced leader and team builder and learn from them.

Team participation and management is a skill requirement for project management. Find a mentor to question. Or find a leader you respect who demonstrates this discipline and follow them as closely as you are able. Emulation will have some trial-and-error aspects, but valuable experience will be earned from the effort.

N-1 AND THE STRETCH

Most business classes, organizational psychology, or an MBA program, at some point, introduce the concept of N-1. This philosophy of labor management involves determining the number of people needed to perform work and providing one less than estimated. The theory being that this will produce tension and stretch the people doing the work to achieve maximized productivity.

Not having enough people is a feature, not a bug.

The implementation of N-1 has practical real-world project management implications. In N-1, all potential project contributors are fully tasked prior to project launch. There are no spare resources or people waiting for work to do. Not only do they have a full-time load, but there are additional stretch items stacked on top. This is the *Balls in a Tube* phenomenon. There are a lot of balls lying around that represent work to be performed and no empty tubes for them to go into. All tubes (contributors) have been assigned their maximum ball capacity. There is no more room. Without acknowledgment of the N-1 environment and a plan for engaging it, the project management experience is problematic.

The phenomena affecting project management in the N-1 environment are not commonly understood. This includes the lack of awareness of the application of N-1 and its effect on project execution. Remember, there is more work than available people, equipment, and money. This is by design. It is a feature of N-1, not a bug. Management has structured it this way. Do not view this as an obstacle. And forget about complaining, N-1 is not going away. Join everyone on board the N-1 train and learn to embrace the suck.

> Join everyone on the N-1 train and learn to embrace the suck.

Navigating N-1 will require excellent communication skills, professionalism, and a positive attitude. All the things discussed in earlier chapters. Everyone you interact with is very busy. They are not looking for problems, complications, or more work. It is important to understand the human part of the contributors you are seeking to engage.

> There are processes and project charters to the left of me, execution to my right, and people here in the middle with me.

N-1 must be considered when strategizing your people approach. There is so much efficiency and synergy to be found in this human space. This is also where the N-1 effect can hopelessly derail your project if you are insufficiently sophisticated in your project management approach. Acknowledgment of the N-1 phenomenon, self-analysis, and skill development is the path forward.

More work than ever can be done

Likely, if you are reading this and engaged in project management, there is literally more work in your task list than you can ever be expected to complete. This result possibly comes from a combination of *Manager's Prerogative* and N-1 implementation.

> The military uses work overload in officer training. Officer candidates will be assigned a long list of tasks and requirements to achieve during their training. They receive demerits for each incomplete or improperly completed task. Enough demerits and you wash out of officer-candidate school. There are literally more things to do than you could accomplish if you gave up sleep and did nothing but work twenty-four hours a day, seven days a week. How do they pass and graduate? By making choices between what can be ignored and what must happen. Take the demerits where they can be sustained and apply effort to the big things that will keep you in the program.

Learn how N-1 works in your organization and use the skills in this book to improve project execution.

What is this matrix everyone says we are in?

The matrix organization is the end result of hierarchical flattening, grouping of similar skill sets as shared resources, and the push for self-organizing teams. The flattening of many companies' hierarchies results in a "pool" of skilled workers who are expected to collaborate effectively without distinct leadership or lines of authority (*The Self-Organizing Fallacy*). Many modern skills can be efficiently shared across the organization. Perhaps a company does not see enough CAD work in individual departments to justify dedicated CAD people on a department-by-department basis and instead implements a "CAD group" as a shared resource.

As in N-1, the human element is amplified in the matrix environment. The practical matrix dynamic is individual contributors with significant autonomy over which tasks they will address.

> The matrix imbues individual contributors with some degree of autonomy over which tasks they will work on.

This autonomy has profound implications for project managers engaging contributors in project work. Take some time to really think about how this unintended matrix autonomy actualizes in the real world. There are different levels of individual discipline and interests. The potential time investment in one-on-one negotiation for a slice of a contributor's bandwidth is real.

As previously explained, with the universal implementation of N-1, everyone is fully loaded and then some with stretch goals. Now combine this with the autonomy of a matrix organization. People with more work than they can ever do, AND they have influence, overtly and covertly, over which tasks they will perform. All with minimal supervision. The introduction and execution of projects in such a contributor environment will not be a straightforward process. Thus, when a new project is introduced, there are no resources available (*N-1 and the Stretch*). And as you work through the process of negotiating one-on-

one with each project contributor, the failure to close the deal with even a single participant will doom the project.

Some contributors interact as if they are not in a matrix organization. Did their supervisor give them the signal to support this project or person? No? Then that contributor does not have time for you. This is not how a matrix organization is supposed to work. That is how a hierarchical organization works. This is where the line in the project management job description "Able to influence others and accomplish goals without legitimate authority." comes from. Successfully managing a project is not just a technical exercise in determining the critical path and executing. **This brief line in the job description defines the people-skill requirement. Hence the need for people-centric project management phenomena skills.**

The realization that the N-1 and matrix phenomena impact project management is an epiphany for a project manager. With the N-1 phenomenon, awareness and guidance on how to engage this more complex environment are critical. Without it, project managers experience endless frustration.

An observation: N-1 and the matrix require project managers with above-average organizational ability and critical thinking skills. Negotiating the crush of N-1 and the matrix while simultaneously delivering real project work is not for beginners.

Some organizations develop robust project processes in an attempt to compensate for N-1/matrix challenges. These well-defined processes still benefit from understanding and acknowledging the people space. People are doing the work. And it is likely the people part was never taken into account in whatever software app, spreadsheet, or written project process that was implemented. Contributors working in the N-1/matrix environment are not looking for another burden. Polite and professional is the rule. Stay positive. Everyone is working hard, and a negative attitude won't help. Don't insinuate or be passive-aggressive. Project management is for adults. Acknowledging the N-1/matrix phenomena and developing a sophisticated approach will improve your project management delivery.

The matrix strikes back (the international matrix)

Outsourcing is the most visible aspect of the international matrix. Grouping skill sets and activities enables moving the work where it is most financially advantageous. The typical N-1 and matrix phenomena remain applicable in the international space. The respective tools implemented may require modification to successfully engage the international matrix.

Collaborating with international contributors is its own unique challenge (*International Communications*). *In Person for Maximum Effect* is not an option. English as a second language can be a real obstacle. *Liability, the Project Killer* and *Angels on a Pinhead* phenomena may be more prevalent. *The Quid Pro Quo Discombobulation* may enter into the equation. You give me something, and I do something for you. This is problematic in the matrix environment. It can also be useful. Facilitating an international colleague's communications and requests within your own region or facility becomes the currency to pay for what you need done. A few exchanges like this can support *Building Bridges*, and you can get past the zero-sum game.

The project management phenomena in the international setting are the same as phenomena everywhere else, though phenomenon emphasis and magnitude may change. Take the time to learn the differences and strategize future approaches accordingly.

Speed is not an N-1/matrix feature

The N-1/matrix project management environment has many useful features. Speed is not one of them. The N-1 work overload, lack of genuine authority when requesting attention from contributors, and the relative autonomy matrixed contributors enjoy in prioritizing tasks slow down project execution. This is not about efficiency or per-unit cost of effort. Assuming the *Angels on a Pinhead* approach is being avoided, N-1/matrix delivers on the promise of maximum output from a minimum of resources. The challenge is in planning and maintaining sequential execution of tasks. Keeping contributors focused and on time is the observed phenomenon.

Frustration at the slow progress of project execution is a common project manager problem. If you have observed it always takes longer to deliver than expected, you're not wrong. Addressing the compartmentalized nature of contributors in a matrix environment and their relative autonomy requires a planned approach (*In Person for Maximum Effect, Be Positive, Constructive Persistence, Balls in a Tube, The 98% Problem, A Little Speculative Paranoia Goes a Long Way, Distraction Elimination, The Easy Button, Building Bridges, etc.*). N-1/matrix environments are awash in people-centric phenomena. Leveraging these opportunities through skill development is the foundation of this book.

Must be able to influence action without direct authority

> Able to influence others and accomplish goals without legitimate authority

The matrix organization often relies on charisma to achieve goals. This is an unreliable and often difficult-to-duplicate approach. This is that line in a job description: "Must be able to influence action without having authority."

Since everyone can't be "insert charismatic person here." What can be done?

This is a sensitive political topic. A private conversation with your supervisor may help illuminate the path forward in a specific organization. Talk about it early and have a plan for influencing contributors. *Defined Escalation* delivered in a calm way is one path to move things forward. Repeated application of this approach will condition colleagues on expectations. Including leadership in key meetings, even if only briefly, is one option. Getting buy-in and support from a well-respected colleague can be the motivation to push others to collaborate.

Don't fall into a *Silver Bullet Improbability* fallacy that there is one combination of effort that always works for all situations. Success in influencing will require a toolbox of approaches. Which one to use will likely be dependent on the situation.

Conclusion

This chapter shares the phenomena observed with the N-1 approach to labor management and the matrix environment from a project management standpoint. Not only are the individual phenomena associated with each concept, but there are also changes to the existing people-centric phenomenon dynamics generated by the two interacting with each other. Acknowledging these phenomena opens a path to developing the tools needed to address their impact on project management. Deployment of an array of skills addressing project management challenges delivers synergistic benefits in the combined N-1/matrix space.

7

PROJECT PLANNING

In the beginning

Beginnings are always difficult. There are two beginnings to plan for in your project management experience. Beginning your career in project management is the first challenge, and it comes with a steep learning curve. The other type of beginning is the start of each new project and its own unique challenges. Both beginnings benefit from advance planning. Hopefully, when you are new to project management, you can start small. Completing projects with an ever-increasing level of complexity and duration. Having early achievements helps build confidence. This is perhaps the best way for new people to start out. Building their skills and confidence in manageable increments.

The beginning of a project can be considered a planned affair, developing a roadmap from a defined scope. This newly minted scope identifies and assigns resource and contributor requirements. Continuation along the planning process leads to determining the critical path. Project execution begins when funding is assigned and the official nod from management. This is the coherent, reasoned, rational process represented in advertisements for project management books and certifications.

The other more commonly experienced project start (based on the author's experience) is more of an *In-Flight Missile Repairman* Scenario. There have been lengthy delays in getting contributors and resources tasked for the project. Even the scope is ill-defined. Then the project is a go and the pressure to complete it is on.

Regardless of which of these scenarios is experienced, acknowledging the importance of a project manager's beginning actions is important. In both cases the first steps must be organized and executed. In the pre-planned scenario this will be a step-by-step process. The second scenario is more akin to triage in a hospital emergency room. Contributors are only available for a short time and must be tasked quickly or be lost.

The phenomenon observed with beginnings is the exponential impact misaligned initial contributor buy-in and tasking have on project success. It's important to align early on with what everyone involved is truly expecting. Just because people accept the project charter or receive an email telling them does not mean everyone has the same understanding.

How does that work? They are all speaking the same language, and the project requirements have been written down, and everyone agrees. Where is the ambiguity?

These are human beings. They all have different experiences and educational backgrounds. Many may speak English as a second language or are at different stages of their careers. There is the interpretation behind the words, where emphasis lies, that must be considered.

Engineers work with data sheets for electrical components. Guaranteed performance characteristics are listed with corresponding values such as "Accuracy: 1%." This is a straightforward representation of how characteristics in a scope document would appear in a project. Everyone reading this understands the goal is 1% accuracy.

Now the questions begin. Is that a six-sigma or three-sigma number? Over what range of measurement? Is that a percentage of full scale or of reading? Is that number made up of gain, offset, and linearity influences? How were those tested? This is all the information making up that 1% number that not everyone may agree on.

When a project begins, key details—even those agreed upon—must be inspected for their potential impact on the project. Look beyond the words for intent: where did they come from, and what is the practical outcome expected? *Bounded Speculative Paranoia* pays off here. Ask questions. Think the project through. Meet with the stakeholders and listen carefully. The goal is to confirm alignment. If everyone involved is not speaking about the project in the same way, the beginning is the time to figure that out. Document and store that information in a place you will remember. Be thorough. Achieving total consensus is not likely. But significant issues are likely to reveal themselves during this process.

> Look beyond the face value of what is represented in a project scope document. Inquire about intent. And then think about how this will be interpreted by contributors.

How many pre-project meetings have begun where everything conceivable is listed on the project whiteboard? Brainstorming generates something more like a tag cloud of a website than the genesis of a project. This is what beginnings often look like: messy.

Stay calm and accept the challenge. Large and/or complex projects are difficult by their very nature. Experience will certainly help, but we all must start somewhere. Remain calm and professional at all times. If you are unsettled, others involved will pick up on that.

Breaking projects up into short-duration efforts (sprints?) helps with individual event-horizon challenges and allows for developmental flexibility as the project situation evolves over time (*Peeling the Onion*). It also addresses the challenge that the longer a project is "open," the more likely it will get changed (*Manager's Prerogative*).

Many projects have an obvious path forward, while others do not. For those with a more complex and nebulous structure, there is an approach called "the object under a cloth." Picture an object on a tabletop, with its shape and physical details covered by a thin, opaque cloth. It is not possible to determine what the object is because the cloth smooths over its physical details, and we cannot just remove the cloth. The object under the cloth represents the project. The goal is to define the project.

The next step is *Asking Good Questions* to gather information about the project. This is likened to driving spikes through the cloth around the perimeter of the hidden object. Each spike pulls the cloth tight, revealing more detail. Skilled execution of this process eventually reveals the shape of the project from underneath the tightly pulled cloth. There are skills and methods of inspection that help with project scope and project launch. Those around intent and interpretation of project definitions help reduce project friction.

The Project Execution Possibilities Curve

Just like the production possibilities curve taught in an economics class, there is a project execution possibilities curve. This is the theoretical maximum rate of project delivery if optimal alignment and efficiencies actualize as planned.

Then there is reality. Project management is executed through processes. Processes are often less than optimal. The greater the process challenge, the less optimal the delivery.

Processes are subject to external influences. Say a critical component holding up the project arrives early, and then the project gets an unexpected leap forward. Or a completion date is discovered to be inaccurate, and now there is a delay. This give-and-take during project execution dynamically moves the completion date relative to the project execution possibilities curve.

Project management experience and skill development improve delivery relative to the project execution possibilities curve. So, stay engaged. Accept the things you cannot change, but be vigilant for those serendipitous opportunities to jump ahead *(Targets of Opportunity)*.

THE CRAP/PERFECTION JUXTAPOSITION

We fired people who kept insisting on perfection.

– Dr. Owe Petersen, former Bell Labs researcher

A failure to achieve perfection can be found in a home improvement project involving tiling a floor. This project included diagonal patterns with multiple sizes of different tiles. Three intricate layouts hand-assembled from a variety of specialized tiles. For the amateur this is all ridiculously difficult, and the amount of time required to finish is beyond the pale. When completed, it looks fantastic. Even if the work is exceptional, it will not be perfect. Its creator knows where all the flaws are. Including that one imperfection where the four corners of four tiles do not exactly line up. No one, other than a tile expert, will see anything other than a beautifully tiled floor.

This particular story is to show how perfection is not a real thing. Perfection is a fallacy. An extreme form of thinking often delivered as a byproduct of the pursuit of excellence. Achieving the best possible outcome balanced against the efficient use of resources is a worthy goal.

Setting a project's sights on perfection is a source of eternal frustration and disappointment.

"We will have a perfect delivery" are famous last words. The real-world delivery spectrum ranges from 100% crap to 100% perfect. At 90% perfection and above, the project's time and resource requirements begin approaching infinity.

Since projects exist for a reason, typically to deliver value, it is safe to assume non-completion will deliver 100% crap. As long as the project is incomplete, the 100% crap outcome is experienced. Only a completed project will deliver value.

Depending on the circumstances, a 5% crap delivery could be a better outcome than the status quo (100% crap). The resources consumed in delivering 5% crap are likely lower than 90% perfect. Delivering 5% crap may reduce the pain in a meaningful way (improvement from 100% crap). A 5% crap delivery can be an intermediate goal while the resources are mustered for a 90% perfect solution (*Peeling the Onion*).

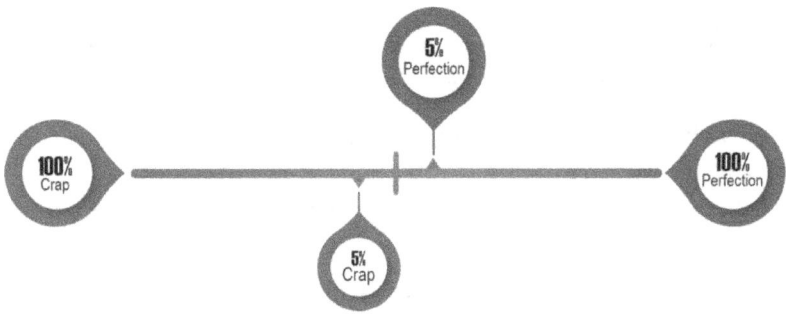

Getting comfortable with a less than 100% perfect delivery saves significant resources. Especially if, at the time of establishing the project scope, not all variables can be properly defined. As long as a less than perfect delivery still delivers useful value of sufficient magnitude to justify the project's expense, it may be considered an acceptable goal.

It is not unusual for a 5% crap delivery to significantly improve the value of a 90% perfect delivery. Things are learned at the 5% crap milestone, and those lessons learned can impact the next sprint to 90% perfect.

> The goal is to meet or exceed expectations, not deliver perfection.

An example is a project to deliver a list of ten potential updates. Delivering a list of nine is still very useful. Having the tenth update at a later time while releasing the nine right away is not perfect, but it delivers 90% of the value.

A project creating a complete list of the components for an automobile would be an example where 100% perfect is required. No one is interested in a car without wheels. In lieu of delivering the infinitely costly perfection is a warranty protecting the buyer. A win-win, so to speak.

The fundamental concept is that many projects deliver value in gradients. Good examples are projects that improve on a current situation. Even small, easy-to-accomplish, incremental efforts deliver meaningful value (there is that sprint reference again). These significant gains from small efforts can be drowned out when there is an imperative for perfect outcomes. Of course, nobody can be faulted for not accepting less than perfection. Which is why some people demand perfection. No explanations are ever needed with perfect. Perfect requires no compromise. Perfect is easy to demand. Requiring perfection is a risk aversion activity (*Liability, the Project Killer*). Requiring perfection and accepting nothing less puts the recipient in a risk-free space. Of course, not much of anything constructive gets done.

The author's goal in writing this book is 95% perfection. Look closely enough, and a defect or imperfection will be found.

The goal of a project manager is to deliver, not find excuses to support a risk aversion addiction. Learn how the steps between 100% crap and 100% perfection in your projects will deliver value.

Welcome to Thunderdome

The most asked question in project management is "When will it be done? Which day?" A reasonable question that is often difficult or undesirable to answer. A project with thirty-plus contributors representing efforts including engineering, manufacturing, compliance, and marketing executed over ten months, and someone wants to know the exact day the project's outcome will be delivered.

There are constructive approaches to convey the needed information in a less confrontational way. Using language like "the anticipated date is" can be a useful tool. Anticipated can be replaced with projected or some similar verbiage. The goal here is not to imitate a politician and prevent accountability. Instead, the goal is to provide space when something interferes with that specific day of completion. And this will happen. Saying "It will be done by close of business on Friday, April 13th" is a declaration that will be challenging to walk away from if it does not work out. Start by avoiding a day. Saying Friday, April 13th, is too specific and likely not to happen. Describe completion in a broader timeframe. "The second week of July" or, even better "July." Even better yet is by quarter, "Q2 of next year." This gives flexibility to handle the last-minute complexities of project delivery while reducing everyone's blood pressure. Another option is to associate a probability with the projected delivery time: "We are perhaps 80% confident delivery will happen in July."

There are three ideas being shared here: don't use overly specific language (e.g., exact date of completion), give a date range, and express probabilities. Project management is in many ways, an expression of maximizing probabilities; this should be expressed in your communications.

127

Get a feel for what level of flexibility your leadership will tolerate. Perhaps another way to say this is what level of realism will be tolerated, as the above reveals much about how the organization delivers on projects.

> Risk aversion, the word "no,", and people's inherent resistance to change are complex challenges.

Now let's discuss the word "no." "No" is the easiest word to say. It delivers a high return in avoidance with virtually zero effort invested. "No" is possibly the most difficult word to overcome. Once a person says no, the effort to change that response to a yes is several orders of magnitude greater than was expended in saying no. Getting past no is better achieved with a plan. An observed phenomenon about no: Some people think they can walk up to someone and just keep talking until they get a yes. Barking at people is not a skilled approach; it is coercion and bullying.

Constructively engaging no and positively achieving a mutually agreed upon yes requires skill. Why skill? Because risk aversion, the word no, and people's inherent resistance to change are complex challenges.

A Lean Six Sigma Green Belt project was launching. There was a technical aspect of the project that required engineering management approval. Performing due diligence and having the needed documentation in order was critical. A meeting was scheduled to present the initiative. The manager said no.

This rejection was accepted gracefully, and the proposal went back to the drawing board. Work was done to strengthen the case, and another meeting was set for two weeks later. This meeting was more successful, and the go-ahead to proceed was given.

The next step in the process required another team to sign off. The initiative was presented with the expectation of a quick approval. The answer was no.

Again, this was accepted gracefully, and the details were further refined. The next meeting scheduled included an ally, the engineering manager who had already given approval. This time, approval was given.

No threats, no escalation, just professional, polite, and systematic engagement. Give the individuals you are seeking approval time to process the ask. Even after they say "no," it is reasonable to re-engage on the same topic after a respectable pause. Do your homework, be prepared, and expect to make several attempts to get past no.

Allies

Alliance-building skills are required to succeed in project management. Allies are those who share information, look out for your interests (and theirs), and are willing to support your project management activities. Allies are critical in bringing groups together. They make introductions and share credibility credentials between strangers. "Bob gave me your name as someone I should reach out to," etc. Mediating misunderstandings often falls to allies. Recognizing the need for allies and how to engage them is another of those important skill sets every project manager needs.

Perform Due Diligence

Due diligence is about gathering information before taking action. Figuring things out, filling in the blanks, confirming requests, etc. Was everything inspected prior to initiating action or asking others? Being able to figure things out, especially the easy stuff, without engaging others reinforces your credibility.

Due diligence also applies to outgoing communications. Are you sure of your response? Really sure? Who is the audience? If you are in error, will it be considered inflammatory? If several levels of management above you are copied on the email, you may want to double or even triple-check. Maybe have a colleague read it over.

There is no such thing as perfect understanding, but has what would be considered reasonable been done? And then double-checked to make sure a simple mistake does not derail the effort?

Expertise in due diligence is important to developing and maintaining credibility. The goal is not perfection, just a solid effort to show that you are paying attention.

ANGELS ON A PINHEAD

The phenomenon: when each new idea is given the green light to proceed, and available bandwidth is never consulted beforehand. Picture a spreadsheet of dozens, if not hundreds, of requests for work to be performed. With available contributors, it could take a decade to complete every task listed. Yet there will never be an effort to rationalize and right-size the list to what can realistically be achieved. More tasks are continuously being added.

A mathematician asked the question, "How many angels will fit on the head of a pin if the first angel is half the size of the head of the pin and each subsequently added angel is one-half as big as the previous?"

The answer: an infinite amount. This illustration represents the time it takes to accomplish anything when this phenomenon appears.

So how does the *Angels on a Pinhead* phenomenon manifest? There are project managers who are tasked with more and more projects. Instead of focusing on the key efforts that are reasonably deliverable, an attempt is made to show continuous progress on all projects. These project managers forget that resources are finite, perhaps limited to ten working contributors, for example. If the project list contains more than ten opportunities to execute, how are the team's efforts to be divided up? Perhaps prioritize and assign one contributor for each of the top ten projects? Maybe double up contributors on certain larger or higher-priority deliverables? Perhaps begin assigning fractions of contributors' time. They can work 30% of their time on one project and 70% of their time on another. As additions are made to the project list, the number of fractions increases in number while the effort available to each task shrinks.

This popular approach to managing workload is a monumental waste of time. The process can be likened to there being a knife of infinite sharpness. Whenever a new task is added, the knife slices off a gossamer-thin bit of bandwidth and drapes it over the new request. Now everyone can say the work is planned for without there being any hope of completion.

A company held management meetings one Saturday morning each month. This gave the team an opportunity to meet without participants being pulled away by day-to-day events in the factory. The team met in a conference room, and at one end of the room was a whiteboard. This whiteboard had a list of perhaps twenty in-progress projects around the facility. Each project had progress notes and an expected completion date.

Each month the project list was reviewed and updated with progress. Prioritization of the projects could be changed and often was. Sometimes those changes were radical, and efforts nearing completion were left stranded.

This exercise in re-prioritization did not follow a rational process. Company resources (money, time, and people) only supported working on perhaps three of these projects at any one time. Yet, in these meetings, prioritization of all twenty was reviewed and changes were made (*The ABCDE Incidence*). Incomplete projects just short of completion would often be reduced in priority (*The 98% Problem*), the efforts and money expended since the last meeting reduced to a loss if the project was never prioritized again. Prioritization often changed based on the need to advance projects that did not demonstrate progress since the last meeting.

Let's read that again: Prioritization increased based solely on the fact that the project did not progress in the last month. A decision not connected to any business case (*Show Me the Money!*).

Instead of delivering any one complete project, incremental progress was spread across the entire list. Result: a year later, nothing much was completed.

This is a glimpse into the nightmare that is the *Angels on a Pinhead* approach to project management. Most humans cannot process more than a few goals at any one time. If the to-do list is too big, contributor and management attentions shift over time. Writing down a list of twenty or more possibilities confuses people and impairs their decision-making. Using *Angels on a Pinhead* with a matrix organization creates a time-wasting engine delivering inefficiency on an epic scale. **It cannot be emphasized strongly enough that *Angels on a Pinhead* is a terrible approach.** It is demoralizing for human beings to work like this. Nobody completes a task well when switching back and forth (*Switching Losses Are Not a Figment of Your Imagination*).

The only benefit to this approach is that a manager can always say "it is being worked on" while being able to demonstrate some incremental progress. There is progress to report at every project update, and no one ever has to deliver the "nothing was accomplished" message. This approach dispenses with efficiency, responsiveness, and productivity for political expediency.

A factor that amplifies the inefficiencies of *Angels on a Pinhead* is that the longer a project is executing, the more likely a meeting will be called and the scope and/or priority tinkered with (*Manager's Prerogative, The ABCDE Incidence*). This possibility increases the risk of delays or outright non-completion. Doing everything at once is the best way to achieve the least progress. If the goal is maximum inefficiency, *Angels on a Pinhead* delivers.

How can this awful phenomenon be prevented from occurring in the first place? Discipline. Applying old-fashioned gratification-delaying discipline. Do not be distracted by the new shiny thing. Have that serious discussion about what is possible and not possible. The ability to stay the course is the skill needed (*Immovable Object*). Prioritize two to five goals and park the rest.

Project delivery will accelerate due to the dramatic increase in efficiency. The bad news is, at some point, management may question why someone unilaterally changed the "doing everything at the same time" approach to a tight focus on a limited number of projects (*Management Cannot Value Something They Do Not Understand*). Prepare for this change-management opportunity. The beginners mistake here is to go straight to management and bluntly tell them they need to limit the number of asks they present to the organization. This is not a constructive approach. Management will be more receptive if improved efficiency is demonstrated, such as lower costs (*Be Positive, Show Me the Money!*). Communication skills will be key to your success.

Addressing *Angels on a Pinhead* is a change-management exercise. There is no silver bullet presented here, but even small incremental improvements will deliver results that can be surprisingly dramatic.

HOOKING ON: GET OFF MY PROJECT

Just as a project is getting off the ground, someone in the organization approaches with this comment: "I heard your project is moving forward. That's great. We have been needing this to happen for a long time. You know what would also be great? Adding XYZ to your project. It is not a big ask."

A project is chartered and organized. The team is on board, and execution launches. When the project begins moving forward, someone will point out how this project is adjacent to another goal. The argument presented is that while the project executes, completing some other related tasks would be easy enough to do.

This is *Hooking On*. The tactic of using a project and project manager's time, energy, and momentum to accomplish other relatable tasks without contributing resources to the main effort. It gives the project manager all the extra work and complexity with no increase in final delivered value.

Catching others trying to attach their work to an already scoped and chartered project is obvious once it is known what to look for. One of the better *Hooking On* repellents is to ask for the business value in hooking on and where the additional resources needed to complete the added work are coming from. A little transparency can make the *Hooking On* attempt go away.

Hooking On is also a version of scope creep. "You're updating those documents? That's great! This has needed to be done for a long time. Did you include these others? It would be good if they all got done at the same time." Management may also see a project moving forward and attach additional deliverables. The siren call of hooking onto a project in motion is difficult to resist for many people looking for a work-around in a matrix organization.

Hooking On can spiral out of control and completely change a project into something that no longer works. Whoever is making the request is taking advantage of the situation for their benefit at the project's expense. This can derail a project as the *Hooking On* requirements begin to expand. It is important for a project manager to be sensitive to this possibility and guard against it.

THE FREE-ASSOCIATION APOCALYPSE

Considering a new project, or some aspect of an existing project, opens up a peculiar door to discussing unconstructive, novel, and never-tried before approaches. During a project's planning stage, there is no cost in adding to its scope, so other people involved will keep expanding it. This means the final deliverable will keep getting more difficult—and likely impossible—to reach.

> Instead of saying no, ask how what is being proposed delivers value worthy of a yes.

This is a tough situation to resolve, especially if the source engaging in this behavior has political underpinnings. No pre-determined, easy-to-use, silver-bullet solution exists.

The best you can do is keep redirecting back to the project's original scope. Ask detailed questions probing the offending request for expansion. Keep pushing for the business value behind the fantasized proposal. Hopefully someone on your team recognizes free association when they see it (*Allies*) and can help keep the creativity focused on practical innovation versus wish-listing.

EATING ELEPHANTS

How does one eat an elephant?
One bite at a time.

– Hindu saying

The work to be done can seem endless. In many ways it feels like someone hands you a fork and points to an elephant and says, "Eat that." Finding even the first step on the path forward seems impossible. *Eating Elephants* is about stacking tasks to the point the end cannot be seen. This level of workload can be demoralizing and unconstructive.

One approach to keeping the forever workload from negatively impacting the team's enthusiasm is to limit the time scope. Only discuss topics within a manageable time frame. Leave the future to the future. Give people the chance to accomplish something. Hold the mega list of tasks to yourself (the project manager). *Eating Elephants* is hard work. Have patience. Get some quiet time. Write things down. Organize things. Address one aspect of the project at a time. Other times, walk away for an hour and do something else. And then come back and re-engage. After some mental inspection, the shape of the project will emerge, and the path forward will become visible. Stay patient; don't give up. You are not the first person to find yourself in the headlights of an oncoming monster project.

Dumping endless, never-to-be-completed work on a single individual is unconstructive. The party line: This maximizes output because there is no possibility of anyone running out of work. Butts in seats looking busy and all that. Make sure no one contributor is getting all the least inspiring work. This can happen with a new addition to the team. The experienced members take everything they least enjoy and create a job from this. Nobody wants that job.

Human beings need to finish what they are working on. Completion is an important part of contributing to a project. There is a shot of endorphins waiting at the end. Be aware of this, and structure the work so they can see the light at the end of the tunnel. **Productivity and engagement soar when completing things is part of the collective work experience.**

Be prepared for your own emotional response to the pile of work. Like so much of what is shared here, experience and awareness combined with communication skills will help with success.

The Long Game

There are aspects of project management that, much like investments, accrue increased value over time, such as building up *Credibility* and developing *Allies*. However, sometimes polite and professional does not get it done. Often a contributor is not on board with the project. Sometimes this is a critical contributor. Regardless of making them aware of the project's charter and visibility, they have other priorities or are not inspired to participate (*Insufficient Gravitas*). Or they may just not like you (*They Are a Peach; Prima Donnas*). This is a tough situation. Such a contributor is typically someone the project manager is unable to compel (*Matrix*) and the only option is a polite and professional request (*Constructive Persistence*). If that does not work, there is a problem. Running to your supervisor or their supervisor will not play out well with your colleagues. Even if that person is then compelled to participate, there is a real possibility that passive-aggressive tactics will follow.

Stay calm and play *The Long Game* (*Run Silent, Run Deep*; *Defined Escalation, Be Positive*). Either this project is going to happen or it's not.

If it is greenlit by your superiors, regular progress reports are likely needed. Never call out the contributor who refuses to engage. Just share in the readout that certain actions are delayed due to conflicting priorities. Give the person who is not performing the opportunity to correct their lack of vision.

Keep the obstacle front and center but low-key. Give them time to figure out the optics that their lack of engagement demonstrates. Wait for your supervisor to ask, and then calmly—and in neutral language—explain the situation.

Eventually, the problem's reluctance will become a bright neon sign flashing, "I am not a team player."

The temptation to *Unleash the Fury!* here will be almost overwhelming. Being forced to play *The Long Game* is the result of a contributor's unprofessional behavior. View these experiences as an opportunity—even a test—of your ability to professionally engage and drive success over time. Even when the inferno of frustration rages.

There are two goals to accomplish in these reluctant-contributor engagements. One is the execution of the current project. The other is to get your long-term relationship on track. Despite the contributor's injection of unneeded drama, it is important to understand that you will work together again in the future. This is why we play *The Long Game*.

OCD as a superpower

A not-uncommon characteristic, certain versions of OCD can be useful in the project management environment. This is not meant as a criticism, nor is the author making a claim to expertise in this area. Only that some people have compulsions around organization and completion that can be more useful than problematic. If someone brings this characteristic as a contributor, perhaps give some flexibility and try to incorporate their OCD as a feature instead of as a bug.

A project is an organized effort to accomplish a task, and even those with OCD need to discipline their talent to be successful. Organization does not just happen. It is a skill to be developed. Observe and learn from others. Emulate what works. Being organized is a continuous improvement opportunity. Invest the effort to develop the skills, and you will never stop finding better ways to structure your tasking activities. And then you can enjoy the efficiency positively impacting your project management efforts.

Organize people

Communication skills are critical when organizing people. Getting contributors on board with the project will be an early project communications opportunity. There is also a constellation of management, interested parties, and gatekeepers, all of whom you must communicate with.

Your ability to organize people will determine if you are able to successfully execute a project. Success hinges directly on your individual communication skills.

Organize information

Projects generate flows of information such as emails, conversations, and meeting minutes. There are official presentations and formal written updates. Information in a project is a lot like the classes taken in college. A subset of all that information will be useful and will need to be readily available sometime in the future. The rest can be discarded. When the need arises, some people become experts in sifting through emails looking for what is needed or scouring whatever storage medium holds the thing they are looking for.

An overlooked project skill is recognizing and organizing the small bits of information shared on a regular basis. These are the insights shared in a meeting. Learn to recognize them when presented and have a method for saving them. One approach is an FAQ or Readme doc with each piece of the puzzle dropped into it. It keeps all the answers in one spot. It takes just moments to save each time, but it delivers big when needed.

The avalanche of project information requires a written record. A memory backup of the project in process. Records of thoughts, spoken details, and short- term tasks to be executed. These should be written down and reviewed/updated regularly. Some prefer typing this into a document on a computer. Others write in a physical notebook.

The author's preferred approach: Manually writing something reinforces memory. Typing, less so. This indicates that the optimal approach is to use a pen and notebook. The written record is the backup, and the act of writing reinforces retention. Over time, it is likely you will develop your own shorthand for your notes. An internet search for typing versus writing for memory retention yields all the needed details. The goal is not to vacuum up everything into your notes. Use good judgment. Put some effort into creating a mental filter to determine what to record.

Make the process your own.

Organize Information is a support function to *Close the Loop*. Depending on the individual, executing the complexities of project management from memory is problematic. People *think* they will remember everything. In practical application, few possess the eidetic memory for such superhuman recollection. Hence, the invention of pen and paper.

Improved information organization can only improve your project execution. Computer files will come at you fast and furious as a project manager. There are those who have become masters of the email search and just look for everything there. An alternative is to assign each project a file folder. While the specific folders created inside the project folder vary by project, they should always follow a similar format.

A philosophy in file naming is to save a new version every time a change is made to a document, spreadsheet, etc. And each of those saves has a date prefix:

1 Jan 23 Important document
The next day, save as:
2 Jan 23 Important document
This new version of a document with the date labels the newest version AND saves older versions. There are times when an older version has information deleted from the newer version. Alternatively, adding a filename prefix of A to a filename pushes it to the top of the folder. A good approach for those files and folders used most often. Create a Z-Archive folder. As documents change from day to day, the old versions are just dropped here to reduce clutter while still being saved for future use.

These approaches incrementally decrease project friction. There is the added benefit of potentially avoiding misunderstandings by having information available with quick and easy access. Make the process your own. Even small changes will win you over to this approach.

Peeling the Onion: An iterative approach

Also called incremental thinking. Building on *The Crap/Perfection Juxtaposition* concept is the iterative or "peeling the onion" approach.

This phenomenon can include several different scenarios. When the goal is not well-defined and an approach is difficult to determine, or the path forward is not visible. There are too many undefined variables, or project information is disjointed and unrelated. Start by writing it all down in any order. After the info dump, go back through it all. The way to organize the information will reveal itself. This is an iterative process similar to brainstorming.

The marketing and communications staff of a large matrix organization were assigned to update product brochures.

141

The team used computer software to create a draft copy shareable to the team. Each team member could make comments on the draft copy, and revisions would be made accordingly. After the first round of comments, a second draft was created based on the comments. This edit-and-update process iterated three times. The final product was much better compared to the first and second drafts.

The supervisor scolded the team for the extra changes. This project was to be a one-edit-and-done task. He had a point. A slam-it-out, single review delivers quick completion.

But is there value with additional polishing stages? The time commitment for a second—or third—review is typically much less than the first. Relative to the value delivered, iterations two and three are likely a good investment. Those customer-facing brochures, when thoroughly edited, will benefit the company for years to come through an improved customer experience.

During the early stages of a project, these iterative reviews deliver significant value. Taking into account what is revealed after the initial establishment of the project and feeding that back into the next round of planning often delivers a positive non-linear ROI as the project progresses.

The peak value is not in the first pass. The second or third pass is when peak value is delivered. After the third pass, diminishing returns are likely realized. Infinite iteration does not deliver infinite value.

> Infinite iteration does not deliver infinite value.

Email writing benefits from the iterative approach. Write that first draft and go back through with a reread. Improved word choice and sentence-structure will be revealed. Spelling errors, duplications, extra words, etc. That second pass delivers significant value in improving the success of the communication. For those critical communications, a third pass is not a bad idea. There are situations where having a colleague read the draft email may even be warranted. Four or more reviews are unlikely to deliver much value.

The complete project picture is often not well understood during the beginning stages. The desired final outcome is clearly understood, but the path from start to completion is unclear. In many ways, this is like a writer starting a new book and staring at that blank page. Time and energy will be inefficiently applied trying to find that perfect path on day one. An author's writing is unlikely to get it correct the first time. Write something down, accept its imperfections, and go to work improving it. Many authors will share how many times they had to rewrite a novel before it could be published.

There are similar parallels in project management. When planning a project, after establishing the path to completion, alternatives reveal themselves. Until the process of planning is performed, the options for improved efficiency are not revealed. Each pass through the planning process continuously improves the outcome. The disclaimer here is that after a point, further iterations will likely deliver dramatically less value.

Management is often not enthusiastic about the iterative approach. They are more aligned with a single-effort-and-done action. The *Making the Sausage* and *Peeling the Onion* approaches have synergies. A developed skill in leveraging the *Making the Sausage* concept can be integrated as part of the *Peeling the Onion* approach. The energy and time savings from *Making the Sausage* help make up for the time lost to a second and third iteration. The final ROI delivered supporting developing this skill combination.

Peeling the Onion is an expert concept because of the subtleties of how many iterations are needed and what is included in each iteration. If this process is new to you, take it in small steps.

Conclusion

This chapter introduced key concepts such as *The Project Production Possibilities Curve* and the *Crap/Perfection Juxtaposition*. *Angels on a Pinhead* is pervasive in the corporate world. Everyone who is made aware of this phenomenon immediately recalls their own experiences with this odious waste of resources. *The Free-Association Apocalypse* rears its head whenever it is possible to add to the project scope without consideration of what the real cost would be. Respecting and addressing project planning phenomena represents a growth opportunity.

8

PROJECT EXECUTION

Project friction

Project friction is the unnecessary slowing of project execution. Less than optimal velocity and quality versus what is suspected is possible or has been experienced in the past? Project friction comes from easily recognized sources such as lack of engagement on the part of contributors. It can take many forms but is generally straightforward to recognize.

SOMETIMES SUCCESS IS JUST SCREWING UP LESS

Striving to be the best is an admirable goal. The best project manager and the best project execution, exceeding all expectations. No one should be faulted for aspiring to deliver a rock star performance, tripping the light fantastic to a spectacular finish.

This kind of thinking tends towards risk-taking and attempting new approaches (*The Silver Bullet Improbability*). This project management style does not take into account project contributors being risk-averse. This approach is also prone to attempting a never-been tried-before type-A activity without considering potential risk. Risk that must be acknowledged to the contributors. Otherwise, contributors may slow down execution due to being uncomfortable with this new, riskier approach.

This is not an argument for never trying new things or never improving performance. Instead, what is being advocated is to not inject an *Inflight Missile Repairman* scenario into a project. New approaches should be vetted before attempting. **High-speed execution is the domain of an experienced team that has worked together before.**

> Experience is what you get when you don't get what you want.

How does this play out in the project management space? Get the project completed while minimizing complications and errors. Keep it simple. Stick to what you know. Don't try to get fancy. Pay attention to the people and practice *Bounded Speculative Paranoia*. The goal is to bring the project to completion.

Rationalizing problems (challenges) in project management

It is a problem when the only acceptable solutions are technology and working harder. These exclude outsmarting the problem. Take a moment to consider the challenge at hand. Is there an easier way? Pause, take a break, and go do something that takes your mind away from the task. Then re-engage.

A manager would leave every day and drive twenty minutes to purchase a coffee. Even though coffee was available at his employer and there were closer coffee shops. When asked why he did this, when many of his colleagues worked through lunch, he replied, "The 45 minutes when I am gone is the best investment of my time the company gets." During this pause from the office grind, it freed up his mind to find solutions. This story gives insight into why remote work may have benefits for roles that require deep thinking.

The initiation of project development is often a messy and disorganized affair. To achieve a more optimized launch will require rationalization of the project structure. Working towards better organizational skills is the path to project nirvana:

➜ Rationalize projects

➜ Rationalize products

➜ Rationalize processes

What does rationalization mean? Rationalization is removing unnecessary complication and distraction. Cleaning away the clutter so the core focus is readily visible. Rationalization is a form of *Distraction Elimination*. It is not an intuitive process. Going back and reordering, categorizing, and removing unproductive elements is a counter to the *The Shiny-Object Distraction*. A ruthless, minimalist approach seeking the core of the project. Rationalization sets the stage for finding the path to outsmarting the problem. This is a skill that gets better every time you use it.

Get on It. Stay on It. – Continuous project focus

If you don't drive your business, you will be driven out of business.

A project management class was offered as an elective in an MBA program. Perhaps halfway through, the class discussion shifted to how to keep a project moving forward. Various software tools and documentation ideas were shared. The discussion was decidedly process-focused: Make sure the contributor team is properly structured. Analyze the project for the critical path forward, analyze contributor loading, and analyze the standard project management process descriptions. The concepts and approaches shared were passive without any engagement or passion. Tools are important; however, in the end, *people* get projects done. **Project execution requires human will driving skills applied to achieve goals.**

> Project execution requires human will, driving skills, applied to achieve goals.

Project management is a leadership role. Leaders must initiate activity. Without this trigger, projects execute inefficiently and/or slow to a crawl. Sometimes they are even completely forgotten. Projects need a driver. And that driver is a human delivering project completion with an aggressive pursuit of the final goal.

Before we go any further, let's define "aggressive" as it relates to project management and completion. Aggressive is not bullying, violent, or rude behavior. Aggressive is the proactive application of energy to motivate people and to drive the project forward. This process remains polite and professional. Successful project management is an aggressive act. Keeping tension on the project and contributors so everyone remains engaged. Someone must take ownership. Passively filling in spreadsheets, sending emails, and holding progress meetings will not efficiently drive a project.

As in all things, moderation and awareness of what the human contributors find acceptable are required. Different organizations support different levels of engagement and aggression. In some cases, those involved derive comfort from "ramrod" leadership, knowing someone is firmly in charge and driving the project to completion. The opposite is when only passive-level engagement is accepted. There is a whole spectrum of project-execution energy between these two points.

Passive-level project management engagement is the slowest and least productive. Unfortunately, this is the turn-the-crank style of project management popular today. A passionless process eventually delivering results with a quality reflecting the minimal human intellect and will input into the process. Engaging and investing in project execution as a discipline and the project itself delivers superior results.

Conductors rule the world

Projects will be made up of many balls in many tubes (*Balls in a Tube*). Orchestrating the forward movement of all of them could be likened to the efforts of an orchestra conductor. The conductor stands in front of the musicians and waves a stick around. That waving of the stick provides cues for the musicians to follow. The conductor is not doing the actual work of the orchestra, making music, but if they do not wave the stick around, the musical results are substandard. This is a people thing and just how things work.

A project manager has an element of conductor in how they guide the collective efforts forward. The critical path is delivered in a certain order and cadence. Communication is used instead of the conductor's wand. There are meetings, messages, and emails confirming balls in tubes are progressing in proper order.

IT'S MAGIC!

It's Magic! phenomenon is when skills, experience, and credibility combine to deliver exceptional project execution performance. There is a situation where the combined understanding of engagement, focus, tension, and people-centric phenomena creates a unique situation. This is where the project manager delivers the impossible while making it look easy. Someone may even remark it looks like magic. Being able to anticipate changes in project characteristics and applying skills to shift the project to a more efficient path is also magic. This positive phenomenon comes from experience. It's a reward earned after years of project management efforts.

A fundamental concept of project management is the critical path. Determining the optimum path to completion is both a goal and a skill. The critical path as a constant is a fallacy. The path to completion changes as the project executes. With experience, insight is developed, facilitating dynamic reorganization of project activities to deliver a shortened critical path. This in turn expands the project closer to *The Project Execution Possibilities Curve.*

As the onion representing the project is peeled (*Peeling the Onion: An Iterative Approach*), so to speak, new options are revealed. Being mindful of these ever-changing opportunities presents the possibility to deliver early, to deliver under budget, or to compensate for lost time.

It is important for the project manager delivering *It's Magic!* to know that others may not understand what they are doing. This is an opportunity for change management and management of expectations.

BALLS IN A TUBE

During a meeting when tasks are assigned, a contributor accepts working on part of the project. The project manager is happy; this is an important task, and the contributor agreeing to work on it is an ideal outcome. The conclusion: it will take perhaps two weeks to complete.

Four weeks later, with no contact or update from the contributor, the project manager follows up. Turns out another task was brought to the contributor. This task was perceived as having higher priority or was seen as more interesting. Maybe the task was prioritized because it was the latest request. Whatever the reason, the contributor has nothing to show regarding the requested ask for the passing of four weeks. Someone more engaged got their work from the contributor done instead.

The project manager assumed, since they had agreed on execution, the contributor was working on the task. This assumption is a common rookie mistake. The world does not work this way.

The explanation suggested here is the idea of the *Balls in a Tube* concept.

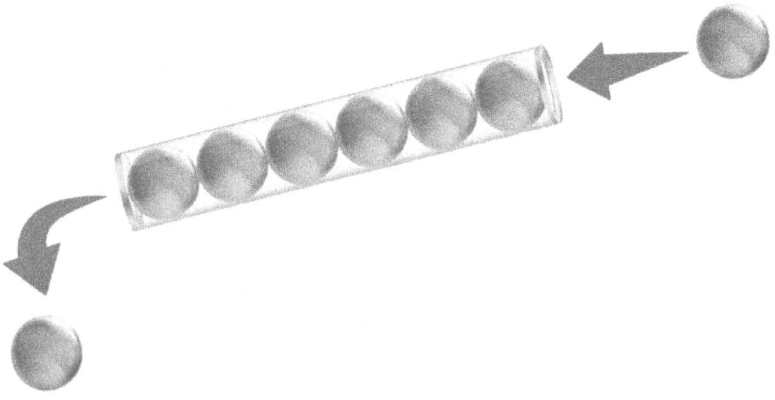

Visualize a tube or pipe capable of holding six golf balls. The balls represent work or actions assigned to a contributor. Based on the N-1/matrix concept shared elsewhere in this book, each contributor's tube is already full of balls. There is no room for your project work.

What to do? Look for a hook. Anything that would motivate the contributor to work with you. For instance, is your project more interesting? Can you present the work as a quick and easy win? Can you show your project has a higher visibility in the organization? Maintain tension on your project elements. Don't allow focus to shift away.

One possible approach is that not all work assignments are created equal. If the discussion is just a brief "Can you work on this?" the contributor's quick reply will be "There is no room in the schedule." But remember, this is a matrix environment, and contributors have flexibility in the prioritization of the work. Opportunities may present themselves after engaging in discussion. (*In Person for Maximum Effect, Credibility, Constructive Persistence*). When successful in engaging a new contributor, a project ball is pushed into the tube. However, another ball falls out the other end. That ball has an owner who will likely try to push their ball back in.

This is where everything can go horribly wrong. Some contributors will agree, sometimes very quickly, to insert the work request into their work queue. They do this because then the requestor goes away. Later, they pop it back out and get on with their life. Please remember to avoid insinuation when addressing these situations. Even in cases where it is 100% positive this happened, just smile and nod. Do not burn a bridge with a valued contributor. Stay focused on the project goals, re-engage the contributor, and get that task back in the queue.

What to do to prevent balls from falling out? Here is a secrets-of-the-universe moment in project management: Check up on your balls regularly. Keep your finger on the ball in the tube. No one should be able to take it out without you knowing. Most project managers move on when they get the ball in place. Stay engaged. Follow up. Check back, and progress will be delivered because the ball stays in the tube.

This also demonstrates to contributors that the project manager is paying attention. This is a useful reputation to have when engaging other contributors on other projects. Condition the team to expect regular follow-up. Be polite and professional but as constant as the North Star. Over time, this consistent approach reduces friction in project management efforts.

Multitasking Can Cause Brain Cancer

It smells in here, and everything's on fire!
And something is biting me! – Erik Lange

The phenomenon of multitasking is at the root of the inefficiencies demonstrated in *Angels on a Pinhead*. Multitasking increases project-execution times dramatically. These losses are real and significant in magnitude due to switching costs. Getting things done requires focus. Alternatively, there is an energy and focus tax on switching tasks. Emails and instant messaging are the worst productivity-tax enablers. Switching focus from a task to an email and back decreases productivity. It is likely not possible to avoid these situations, because most people reading this book perform literally hundreds of different tasks in a day. Like the other project-management phenomena shared, the goal here is awareness. Awareness of the cost of task switching will help you identify the problem and keep the multitasking under control.

Some tasks require exceptional focus, time, and imagination to complete. Learn to identify and plan for these, because to achieve a high-quality delivery, these high-talent-input tasks should be scheduled so that they are not interrupted. The term for this is deep work. Start a task; finish a task. This is the most efficient way to execute tasks within a project. Often this is not possible, but acknowledge the challenge and leverage this understanding to improve project success.

LIABILITY, THE PROJECT KILLER

It is easier to ask for forgiveness than permission. – U.S. Navy Rear Admiral Grace Hopper

---

Most people are uncomfortable executing the above quote in their work. This is a sane response to situations with too many variables. Alternatively, if the project manager has significant experience and understanding of the limited outcomes and the probabilities of those outcomes, then asking for forgiveness is an option.

Liability can be a contributor-participation killer. High perceived liability (*Perception is Reality*) can trigger risk-avoidance behavior, complicating project participation. No one wants to be persecuted for negatively impacting a project.

Contributors to projects are mindful of the liability risk associated with a task. This consideration of potential negative outcomes influences their enthusiasm. There are those who play it very safe and only move forward with a sure thing, and then there are the foolhardy. Unique to each contributor, risks and rewards are calculated based on project topic interest and personal risk threshold. Most contributors never verbalize this mostly subconscious process.

Risk aversion can drive bizarre behaviors that are less than constructive.

Risk aversion can be identified by the use of everyone's favorite risk-avoidance word: No. There is nothing fundamentally wrong with saying no. It is good to have people in the organization who can deliver this word. If engineers do not say no, all kinds of bad things happen. No is the word used to prevent bad choices and undesirable outcomes. Without no, bridges fall down, planes fall out of the sky, and other bad things happen. These are just a few examples of what happens when someone does not say no when appropriate. Using "no" to drive the risk to zero is not an appropriate use of this otherwise useful word.

> "No" is the easiest word in the English language.

Now, what are some signs of liability concerns? Contributors engaging in unconstructive communication behavior is the most common. Instead of a meaningful discussion, there will be a continuous re-inspection of project details and questions answered with questions (*The Circular Firing Squad*). Including an unexpectedly large number of people in every meeting or copied in every email is another. Sometimes contributors continuously request further clarification, or they are the opposite and are evasive in every interaction. Another sign is avoiding delivering a conclusion or assigning responsibility. Some people will keep bringing up details and related topics while avoiding defining a path forward. Each of these manifestations of risk avoidance could be described as the opposite of decisive. If decisiveness and conclusions remain elusive, risk aversion may be the reason.

A project manager will be on their own figuring out when risk aversion is happening. Just asking does not work. Most people do not even know why they are reacting the way they are.

Mitigating project contributors' perceived risk is a skill. Yes, perceived. The risk may or may not be real. Its actual existence is not relevant to the contributor. Their perception is what must be addressed (*Perception is Reality*). The suggested tactics to get past the risk-aversion shenanigans are transparency and transference. Acknowledge the concerns. Share your understanding. Don't point fingers or try to shame them. This is an opportunity to show leadership and advocate a constructive path forward.

After identifying and publicly sharing the challenge, the quickest way to get things back on track is to transfer the risk to the project manager. Put it in writing or accept it verbally. "I, the project manager, am requesting this action and fully understand your concerns. Regardless, we are doing this anyway."

An actual approach will be less melodramatic, but the fundamental goal is to take away the contributor's responsibility for the risk. If something goes wrong, it is not their problem. Remember, this is about their perceived risk. In many cases, the project manager is accepting liability for a risk that does not exist.

> Contributor participation secured at zero cost. Infinite ROI achieved!

Mitigating risk can have dramatic results. It can transform delay tactics into full-blown enthusiasm. The contributor wants to participate and do the work. They just do not want to be liable if something turns out less than ideal. The project manager will need to be confident to pull this off. It's definitely not an approach for a novice.

A long-term benefit of risk mitigation is the positive effect it will have on your credibility and the willingness of others to work on your projects. They know an experienced, steady hand is guiding the project.

> There will be no scapegoating or persecution of the innocent. There is power in this.

Mastery of managing project liability can make the impossible possible. Successfully engaging this phenomenon requires excellent planning and communication skills and a well-developed ability to gauge risk. Incorrect execution can have grave consequences.

THE QUID PRO QUO DISCOMBOBULATION

There are those who believe that unless you can do something for them, there is no motivation to participate. It is logical, after all. If someone goes to a store to purchase a candy bar, the store receives money in exchange. Should not the same be true for the contributor's valuable time? The contributor's input is required for the project, so what will be exchanged for that input? The answer is nothing. At least not in the context they are requiring.

A quid pro quo shakedown is void in a corporate matrix environment. The employer has already compensated them for their efforts while allowing for flexibility in task execution. The leadership will set the priorities for project execution. Failure to deliver can be handled by them.

Keep things polite and professional. Stay engaged with the individual. Document and communicate (*Defined Escalation*). Regularly update your leadership. If the contributor's inaction eventually results in delays, it will fall on them to explain.

Insufficient Gravitas

It starts like this: A supervisor assigns a project. It may be a straightforward, short-timeframe deliverable. Find something out, update a document, or make a presentation.

The contributor who needed to perform the work has been with the company a long time. The project manager's request for assistance is polite and professional. The ask is well-defined and straightforward. The time required to complete it is short. But they are not responsive. An email requesting an update is sent. No reply. A meeting invite is scheduled. The contributor declines. Calling them on the phone and instant messaging them yields no progress. Engagement remains elusive. No matter the approach, there seems to be no way to get the contributor engaged.

Stay professional. Then engage your leadership. There are legitimate times, after all other approaches are exhausted, when asking for support is reasonable. But this only works if you are calm, and professional, have documented the lack of engagement, and have a clearly defined ask.

Sometimes the engagement needed is just copying your boss, or their supervisor, in the email or a CC to a meeting or inviting more senior people to a meeting. If this happens often enough, management will figure it out.

THE ABCDE INCIDENCE: WANDERING FOCUS AND CIRCULAR PRIORITIZATION

A common experience in project management is having priorities change in response to new information. Many organizations have project lists that are reviewed, weighted, prioritized, updated, and altered on a regular basis.

A phenomenon often seen repeated over and over is described below:

A project execution list is currently in this order: A B C D E.

A week later, new information, a customer complaint, a new initiative, etc. draws leadership's attention. The priority is rearranged slightly: D A B C E.

The teams working on B and C respond to the change by pointing out the importance of their projects. Compromises are made, and the order is updated: B C D A E.

The changes to the order alter some of the weighting and priorities, and a previously settled fifth-place project has its position upgraded, resulting in another new order of projects: E B C D A.

A manager returns from vacation, and after a week of digging out, he learns of the priority changes while he was out. A meeting is called to address his concerns. The newly updated project order: A B C D E.

Numerous time-consuming meetings, jockeying, emergency evaluations, responses, negotiations, and so many emails later, and the project order ends up back where it was originally.

These situations are driven by the imperative that someone be seen taking action. In the above example, multiple actions were taken. Priorities were changed several times. Many expensive hours were wasted. The opportunity cost alone is offensive to consider. It is a truly appalling and irresponsible waste of resources.

The goal here is not to promote inflexibility or prevent change but to share what is not often acknowledged. Management may have good reason for making priority changes. However, if the priority changes become circular, some explanation may help with morale.

Changing priorities confuses those executing projects and wastes resources. Psychologically, it is hard on the team. Consider the resources conserved and opportunity costs avoided by acknowledging these unconstructive exercises.

WHERE THE HELL ARE THE GOALPOSTS GOING? - WHIPZILLA

At the end of a project, when completion is imminent, someone gets cold feet. A manager, contributor, or possibly even someone not directly related to the project. A panicked inspection of the final project deliverables will be initiated, often with feverish missives about how there is a problem. Was anything missed? Are there aspects to be crammed in at the last minute? Will perfection be delivered (*The Crap/Perfection Juxtaposition*)? Aspects of the project are hastily reviewed, and risk aversion kicks into overdrive. Last-minute changes will be hammered into the project. The almost completed, elegant, on-time delivery just evaporated. This behavior is classic risk aversion.

Knowing in advance that this phenomenon may occur is a sign of experience. Be careful with what information is shared just before project completion. This is not a recommendation to mislead or obfuscate. Just be judicious in your language. Most stakeholders are pleased when a project is delivered. There are a few who are paranoid that some detail will come back to haunt them. This fear can spiral into paralysis by analysis and inject extreme risk-aversion behavior. Make sure other, possibly stoic, people are involved in these communications (*Allies*). Hopefully there are others who can provide guidance and/or run interference, assisting in preventing delivery derailment.

How to fend off these last-minute attempts to extend the project time? The first method is to be transparent regarding risks associated with last-minute changes. Delays and uncertainty inserted just as the project is closing are not without cost. Share those costs. Don't use inflammatory or confrontational language. Just lay out the facts in neutral terms.

The second method is to define the opportunity cost in money. As an example, lost potential delay in sales (*Show Me the Money!*) is a strong method to end needless dithering at the end of a project. Define what the project will not deliver. This may improve the pushback position when goalpost-moving risk aversion kicks in. Most projects are clearly defined in what they are to include and/or accomplish. Take some time to think about what the project will not be delivering. Perhaps there are things that others may inject at inopportune times. Thinking about those limits ahead of time and the associated costs and risks is a forward-thinking skill to help stop unconstructive goalpost moving. Mastering this phenomenon is an opportunity to develop your project manager prowess and grow from a rookie to a maestro.

THE 98% PROBLEM/FINISH WHAT YOU START

There is an inevitable shift in focus just before the project reaches its conclusion that should be anticipated. This phenomenon occurs in most human endeavors. It appears to be hardwired into people to start ramping down and shift focus as an activity draws near its conclusion.

Grit is the term for finishing what you start, delivering a sustained effort. Project managers need a lot of grit.

This could be likened to an inverse of the Zeigarnik effect. Instead of anxiety to complete and finalize the effort, there is a "close enough" loss of focus.

An urban legend, perhaps, but there is a story of a hiker who had mapped out a trail in Death Valley. His goal was to hike this path in the minimum time he could possibly achieve. Essentially competing against himself. The challenge was not just speed over distance. This was Death Valley, and the high temperature was a factor. A hiker in this environment had to drink water, a lot of water, to survive. The hiker was able to calculate the exact amount of water he would need. Less water meant less to carry. Less to carry meant a shorter trip time. After completing the hike, they apparently stopped for a moment within sight of his vehicle. As he cooled down from exertion, the blood in his dehydrated body thickened, and he died. He was found dead, in sight of his car, within which gallons of water waited.

The phenomenon observed: It is apparently human nature to be distracted or relax just before crossing the finish line. It is a human phenomenon to pause before completing a task, and pause is dangerous. In the story above, it was fatal. In project management, it can prove fatal to the project. Contributors who take a pause as the end is in sight open themselves up to distraction.

When a project nears completion, there will be a collective shift in focus (*The Event Horizon*). Everyone involved will begin looking to their next activity. This will result in a dramatic decrease in the project's forward momentum. Without foresight and discipline, that last 2% of the project will take as long to close out as the first 98%.

What to do? Watch for the change and be ready to mitigate. Drive projects to a complete delivery. The project manager does not have the privilege of shifting focus as the collective effort concludes. Stay engaged as the project nears completion (*Get on It. Stay on It.*). Have good visibility to whatever makes up that last 2%. Clearly define these final responsibilities and deliverables. Increase the tempo of updates. The project manager's engagement ramping up at the end of a project will help keep the greater team on task.

Switching Losses Are Not a Figment of Your Imagination

Real work that adds value in an organized process requires skill and energy. The amount of energy, focus, tools, space, and collaboration needed to complete a project represents an investment, a store of value. That store of value to some degree evaporates when the project is halted and then restarted or if contributors are switching between different assignments. This breaking of execution rhythm is referred to here as switching losses. These dreaded switching losses are what make the *Angels on a Pinhead* approach the abomination it is.

For more information on the horrific waste that is switching losses, perform an internet search for Dr. Gerald Weinberg on the topic.

Over time, allowing projects to execute and complete while minimizing switching losses dramatically increases the organization's overall project capacity. As a project manager, every effort to keep switching losses under control can only improve project execution velocity.

HOW FUN AND UNFUN IMPACT PROJECT DELIVERY

Most tasks within a project involve actual work. Sometimes these activities are not terribly stimulating, but they make up much of the employment experience. As adults, we execute tasks of this nature regularly without a second thought.

Then there are those unstimulating tasks, onerous and undesirable, whose only reward is their eventual completion. These are projects so ugly, so brutal, and so demanding, it is unlikely anyone wants to get involved.

163

One observed phenomenon is when a project manager is completely honest and transparent while communicating onerous tasks, it increases contributors' buy-in. Acknowledging the magnitude of the ask builds credibility. It also emphasizes the importance of the contributor as the only person who can make the difficult possible.

There was an opportunity to improve a piece of industrial equipment in a facility that thermally processed metals. The equipment being updated was critical to plant operation and could only be shut down for twenty-four hours maximum. The available workforce was able to do the work, but it was estimated to take at least twenty hours.

The team was gathered together, and the request was presented. It was emphasized that due to the long duration, participation was not a requirement. The reality of the situation was shared up-front. The work would be physically demanding, dirty, and just unpleasant. This frank sharing of the work requirements depressurized the team's anxiety. Everyone knew what a monsterous undertaking was ahead of them. The unspoken concerns had been spoken and confronted as a team. Twenty-two hours later, they finished. It was an accomplishment the team was proud of. A challenge overcome together.

· · · · ·

A similar story, perhaps more of an urban legend, is when Sir Ernest Shackleton advertised in the *London Times* for men to join his next Antarctic expedition. "Men Wanted: For hazardous journey, small wages, bitter cold, long months of complete darkness, constant danger, safe return doubtful. Honor and recognition in case of success." According to Shackleton, the response was of such magnitude it was as if the whole of London wished to join.

These examples show approaches to characterizing less desirable activities as unique challenges. It would be wise to sparingly draw from this well. Otherwise, you risk team burnout. Regardless, when the truly awful injects itself, there is a potential path forward.

Reducing Project Friction—The project death march condition

Keeping projects from slowing in execution or renewing a project to a faster pace of delivery are common project management goals. Even better is recognizing opportunities to further accelerate an otherwise healthy project.

Common reduced execution contributors:

- An important requirement was not defined properly
- The team does not include a needed contributor
- Insufficient resources
- Nothing is ever complete (*Where the Hell are the Goalposts Going?*)

An equipment updating project stalled while waiting on an electronic device installation. The electrician installing the equipment kept asking for another day or two to complete it. Eventually another expert was engaged to bring the project to a conclusion. This was an example of *The Light-Bulb Electrician* situation hindering AND confusing the project effort.

Just as there are undesirable impacts on project execution, there are many potential project accelerators. These are how to build a project management execution machine:

- → Long-term allies
- → Experienced team
- → Right tools for the job
- → Credibility

➜ Communication skills

Having allies or engaged leadership participating at critical times focuses the greater team and lends credibility to the project manager's efforts. A project manager with a track record of successfully delivering will have greater buy-in from contributors. There is also the understanding of participating in what is likely going to be a good outcome based on the project managers' experience.

DISTRACTION ELIMINATION

A plant engineer had multiple projects in motion and six direct reports to execute them. His manager was fixated on old, unused equipment. The belief was that money could be saved by pulling spare parts from the junkyard. The plant engineer knew it was all valueless garbage. Unfortunately, this was not a constructive message to share with the manager. The junkyard of long-dead machinery proved itself a distraction over and over again. Staff were pulled from other duties to try and salvage a part from a pile of junk. The manager would grab one of the plant engineer's direct reports and reassign them to trying and resurrect a long-dead machine. That direct report would then not complete tasks previously assigned. There was no constructive way to deflect the manager's attention.

That left what is perhaps a passive-aggressive solution: Eliminate the distraction. Every day for several months, the plant engineer started the morning with a cutting torch and a fork truck, spending a few hours filling dumpsters with scrap steel. With the junkyard gone, the manager stopped re-tasking people. Distraction eliminated.

The likelihood of a distraction causing a problem within your project depends on the individuals involved. Some people lose focus easily. Others are sensitive to only certain distractions. Once you acknowledge the phenomenon in general, the skill to see when it is happening will manifest naturally.

Torpedoes In the Water—Sub-projects in motion

There is a project management tactic that can help reduce the number of tasks requiring immediate attention. Many tasks require regular engagement on the part of the project manager, but then there is a handoff to another contributor who must execute before the project manager must touch that aspect of the project again. Sometimes this is called "handing off," or "the ball is in someone else's court," or less positively, "tossing it over the wall."

A variation on this is called "torpedoes in the water." This is taken from old war movies where a torpedo in the water has to propel itself a significant distance from when it is released to when it reaches its target. During that run time, there is nothing more to be done but wait.

A useful approach is to perceive the time span others are actualizing part of the project as a feature, not a bug. Set up a project effort, remove obstacles, complete any needed input, and then schedule the next efforts. Hand off the task to the contributor. There will be a relatively predictable amount of time before the project manager will need to re-engage with that responsibility.

While the torpedo tasks are running through other contributors, it frees up the project manager's time and energy to focus on other tasks. Now that aspect of the project can run autonomously for some time. This is a great way to set up the progression of multiple tasks that are relatively short in duration (weeks, maybe a month) while freeing up your time for the more complex tasks.

Torpedoes In the Water has a defined beginning and destination understood by the project manager. Even though there is no direct input to the work in progress, you're aware of the next milestone, and re-engagement is expected.

Targets of Opportunity

Put everything in priority order. Establish project priorities early because knowing their relationship to the critical path puts you in a position to take advantage of targets of opportunity. Prioritization of tasks is important when determining if the correct order of tasks is being actualized. Here is where those developed *Asking Good Questions* skills will deliver. Get the information needed to make decisions and define the path forward.

There are times when the planets align and people, equipment, time, money, etc., become unexpectedly available. If the work to prioritize everything has been done, identifying these situations is more likely. Don't hesitate to take advantage of these rare opportunities. Keep the project organized, with a defined scope and requirements and a documented path forward. Then, when serendipity strikes and resources are unexpectedly made available, execute. The possibility then exists to deliver something normally impossible otherwise *(It's Magic!)*.

Another target of opportunity is the completion of short time-duration project tasks. Delivering a win like this provides a sensation of forward motion to contributors and management. Contributor morale is boosted because things are getting done. The leadership sees progress, which is always great. Multiple actions are closed out early, decreasing project complexity. The project manager now has a better-defined scope for the project and increased confidence. If these project opportunities present themselves, take advantage. Everyone benefits.

All aspects of the project will likely not advance simultaneously. There may be parts of the project that feel almost independent from the main effort. This independence is a potential opportunity to execute and deliver something with minimal complexity. This is good for morale and the overall appearance of the project. Close out those short, easy-to-deliver opportunities early.

Chaos management

There will always be some level of chaos in the project management environment. Critical thinking skills will support the decision-making required to determine when chaos will negatively impact the project and if some aspect or level of chaos should be tolerated.

To be sure, uncontrolled chaos and successful project execution are, however, mutually exclusive.

Here are some "chaos level test" concepts:

◊ When everything is important, then nothing is important.

◊ There needs to be normal work. Perhaps a definition or understanding of what normal is

◊ Contributor availability conflicts

◊ *Switching Losses Are Not a Figment of Your Imagination* is impacting project execution.

◊ Definition of the project is unclear or in continuous flux *(In-Flight Missile Repairman)*

If everything is a "10" in importance, there will be problems. Either there is serious technical debt overload and resource allocation is insufficient (*Angels on a Pinhead*), or there is an opportunity to re-evaluate priorities. Painting every project and/or aspect of a project with a broad "critical" brush can lead to poor outcomes as resources are squandered rushing about. Under these conditions, project execution takes on a brittleness or stretched feel.

How to differentiate and quantify project priorities? Document the project to detail each part, which removes the ambiguity delivering the chaotic label. Then reference the money value for each project. If there is a business case associated with the project, the needed information should be readily available. Once the top-line or bottom-line impact of the different actions has been clarified, much of the chaos falls away.

Reaching out to leadership for guidance in this space is reasonable, perhaps even welcome (*Show Me the Money!*). *Perform Due Diligence* and clearly define the ask and the business case. Be transparent about the challenge. The feedback needed on priorities may come back quickly and decisively.

Conclusion

This chapter delivered concepts and paths forward to constructively reduce project friction. *Get on It. Stay on It. i*s a core project manager philosophy, or it should be. Numerous observed people-centric project management phenomena were shared. Take this shared knowledge and start making things happen.

9

PROCESS & PROJECTS

Project management is often executed through processes. Perhaps the process is straightforward, such as a measurement followed by an adjustment, or it may be a multi-step, complex effort following a detailed guide or even a sophisticated, networked software application. Regardless of the specifics, there are people-centric phenomena that arise during process execution. Visibility to their existence and the understanding of some of the more common ones shared here will only improve project execution.

Phenomena around process can be the most difficult to identify and the most difficult to address. This difficulty is because they are not part of the actual project but something the project engages with.

THE PROCESS APOCALYPSE: FRANKENSTEIN PROCESSES

Undefined or poorly defined processes derail a project. Projects all make sense in the beginning. They start out with good intentions: a well-thought-out effort addressing a compelling need. The same is true with processes.

A spreadsheet was created for a quoting process that included pricing custom or semicustom systems made up of complex subsystems and components. All the work was done in spreadsheets. The process was straightforward: put quantities in certain cells, and the spreadsheet math does the work. The final sales price is the output.

The spreadsheet contained a small selection of standard offerings. All other systems were à la carte with many options. The idea behind the standard system was for it to be a lower cost option versus à la carte, with the standard package being the most popular selling product as an established system. It was advertised as shorter delivery and less upfront engineering, making it a quick and easy choice.

While reviewing the spreadsheet's outputs, a comparison between the standard offerings and the à la carte ones revealed the à la carte was less expensive. With the customer tendency toward getting a standard quote and an à la carte quote, the optics on the approximately 25% premium for the standard offering was a problem. Customers did not react favorably to what had been advertised as the less expensive standard option being 25% more expensive. The situation had all the characteristics of a bait-and-switch.

First thought: What a brilliant sales strategy to increase profits! Steering customers to the standard offering through the implication it is the easier, faster, regularly manufactured version (implying lower risk) and then charging a premium in their ignorance. Perhaps it would have been a brilliant strategy if it were true. Again, customers had the systems quoted both ways and would share their confusion.

Upon further inspection, it was determined this spreadsheet had passed from owner to owner, each in turn making changes to the formulas involving pricing. The result was an impenetrable morass of interlocking, difficult-to-explain math formulas arriving at an irrational pricing structure. This is how Frankenstein processes are created.

This dysfunctional outcome was not arrived at by design. There was no malicious intent. Regardless, a point was eventually reached where the process failed. Or at the very least, uncertainty and inefficiency were added to the point that they virtually killed the activity it was supposed to govern.

When a project requires such a process, it's important to identify the malfunction before time is lost. This is where *Bounded Speculative Paranoia* can help. Perform rationality tests on numbers and outcomes. Question if the process is making sense; don't just assume.

Unrealized potential as far as the eye can see

Be prepared to identify process apocalypse scenarios as they occur. A real-time strategy to communicate and provide guidance to the team will be needed. The goal here is to acknowledge the phenomena and guide the project through the process obstacles with minimum losses.

Underperforming processes are everywhere. A dose of skepticism and a questioning attitude will pay dividends by preventing lost time and resources grinding through something that is sub-optimal or even broken.

THE FRANKENSTEIN DYSFUNCTION IN REAL-TIME

Don't become an inflight missile repairman

A project manager will likely not have visibility to a Frankenstein process until after the project is executing through it. Real-time identification of dysfunctional processes is critical. Otherwise, frustration at the inability to achieve goals will begin to impact project focus. No one wants to work on a death march of a project where everyone is fighting process instead of doing actual work.

Be aware of the existence of *The Process Apocalypse* phenomenon, and have the tools ready to prevent the situation from speed-bumping the project. This is not about *if* it will happen. This is about *when*. Knowing this will happen—and that it is not unique to your personal experience—reduces the stress and anxiety when it does. Success lies in developing the tools to engage and resolve the challenge.

The visibility that being a project manager gives to all aspects of the project is not a shared experience with contributors. As project manager, it is possible you will be the only person to identify the process as the problem. Most project participants are doing work, not determining whether the effort is delivering the desirable outcome. Sensitivity to the differences between a higher-than-expected workload versus a poorly structured process is key. Adding people can address both gaps. But only one of them efficiently delivers added value.

Inefficient processes are legion

Superstitions are alive and well in the corporate world. Belief in long, meaningless-but-still-used processes whose origin is long forgotten but still followed because people think it is necessary.

> Process insanity: the belief that a broken/flawed process actually works.

Created long ago, their origins shrouded in the mists of time, many processes governing corporate activity are legacy creations. Although everyone executes through processes, no one is reviewing, updating, or innovating processes.

Processes are often built from older processes, with no critical review performed on their arcane machinations. Working these ancient, poorly documented, and equally poorly understood work streams is the ongoing nemesis of project management.

Why do these inefficient, energy-sucking fossils still govern so much in the corporate world? Because changing them is fundamentally unfun, high risk, and high effort. The only reward: a thankless change-management effort. No manager ever maxed their bonus addressing legacy processes.

THE DERATED DERATE OF A DERATE: PROJECT INSPECTION

Say a cabinet requires ten screws to put together. What happens if one of them is missing and only nine are shipped? Or the final customer drops one and it rolls away and they cannot find it? Shipping eleven screws with every cabinet solves both problem scenarios for the cost of a single screw.

Then at shipping, the bag of eleven screws is thrown in the box. The person who does this is worried if one bag is enough. It would be terrible if they did not have enough screws . . . So, they toss in another bag, just to be sure.

At the distributor, there is a meeting about customer complaints around missing screws. So, they have extra bags shipped in, and every cabinet going out will have this extra bag taped to the box.

The customer gets the cabinet and when they are done assembling it, they wonder if something is missing because they have all these extra screws.

This phenomenon is the "more is better" approach. It can be applied to so many aspects of project management where contributors add some extra just to be sure.

The name for this phenomenon came from the author's experiences with electrical components. The manufacturer says the component is rated for 85 degrees Celcius. The company building a product that includes this component inside derates it to 70 degrees Celcius, for increased product life and reliability. The customer gets the product and won't use it above 50 degrees Celcius, to achieve maximum life. Thus, the derated derate of a derate occurs. The joke is on both the final product manufacturer and the end user. Because the component manufacturer specs the reliability at six sigma survival for many, many years at 85 degrees Celcius.

Don't pile on or add margin just to be careful. Know what is needed and just do that. As a project manager, it would be unreasonable to expect inspection of every dimension, quantity, and performance spec. Instead, watch for unconstructive behavior, risk avoidance, or overcompensation. Resolving and rationalizing only a single *The Derated Derate of a Derate* in a project is a big step up in project value delivery.

IN-FLIGHT MISSILE REPAIRMAN

During project execution, a bad process presents itself. This is when a process problem becomes visible and the idea to update the process is brought to the project participants' attention. A bizarre form of *Hooking on* may be injected where the energy of the project is leveraged to fix the process while simultaneously working through the project through the process. This attempt to fix the process during a project is *In-Flight Missile Repairman* phenomenon.

This distraction of fixing the process becomes the project focus instead of bridging process issues to keep the project moving. Fixing a process is a project in itself. Do not subject your project to the scope creep that process updates become. Do not open the door to complexity-focused people winding up a complicated upgrade to the process (*Smart People Think Complicated Is Fun*).

There is a second kind of *In-Flight Missile Repairman* project management phenomenon. This second version is when a project begins execution before the project structure is in place. Work begins before the defined project deliverables have been documented. The project manager will be pressed to keep contributors fully loaded while simultaneously trying to figure out the project fundamentals. This will likely lead to less-than-optimal outcomes. Avoid either kind of *In-Flight Missile Repairman* experience.

Make it fit?

Now to contradict what was just said in *In-Flight Missile Repairmen*. Sometimes fixing the process is required to move a project to the next step. When this happens, here are some options to try.

Option 1: Fix it permanently. The energy cost to make do and push the project through without a proper process fix means the next time the process is used, the high energy cost will still be there.

Option 2: Viewing poorly defined and poorly understood processes as opportunities. Use the lack of process definition to minimize complexity and accelerate the project. Figure out the minimum requirement needed to honor the process and execute.

This option 2 approach is not about cheating or a lack of integrity. This is about rationally dealing with the process's poor fit, lack of rigor, obsolescent aspects, and/or right-sizing the process effort to the task at hand.

What is really needed? It is important to meet the minimum process requirements in a way that can be explained. This will protect your credibility. Then eliminate the nonsensical and time-wasting make-more-work steps that add no value. Be transparent (*Management Loves Surprises!*). Document and communicate what is being done.

The process money machine

There is a continuous improvement opportunity not often realized. For those with masochistic tendencies and iron will, improving legacy processes offers an opportunity to satisfy a continuous-improvement itch. Finding these nuggets of pure gold in process improvement will not be difficult. Once the value is discovered, the magnitude of the dollars returned to the company's bottom line will be impressive. Reduce complexity, eliminate unnecessary activities, document, and clarify. Expertise in this rarified space will deliver value. With experience, higher-value improvements will become apparent.

Looking for bad processes is something most do not voluntarily gravitate towards. However, once the idea to look for bad processes manifests, the actual work of inspecting and finding them is easy. Bad processes are everywhere. The challenging part is the actual work of updating and fixing bad processes.

Passion for the process and discipline

Project management requires determination, focus, a desire to see the project through to completion, and a passion for delivering a completed project. Engaging at this level can be challenging if the subject of the project holds no interest for the project manager.

The solution here is to focus on a passion for the process, not necessarily the subject of each project. The project manager's process involves structuring the project. Efficiently executing through the steps. Anticipating what can go wrong and making contingency plans. Creating innovative solutions when the project starts to go off the rails. Successfully engaging contributors and ensuring a final, elegant delivery. Leveraging newfound awareness and skills in managing people-centric project management phenomena. These skills and processes become the passion.

Conclusion

Process challenges can negatively impact project execution. Anticipate their existence and establish criteria for whether to fix the process or work through it.

Certain peculiarities exist in the project management and process space. *The Derated Derate of a Derate* and *In-Flight Missile Repairman* scenarios are expert-level phenomena. Identify them, and your project's level of success will improve. Working processes are as valuable as a well-defined critical path. Develop a mastery of process and enjoy the benefits.

10

TIME-FRAME REFERENCE & EXPERIENCE

> Bandwidth is not infinite. Plan
> accordingly.

During a project's genesis, investing thought into managing knowns and unknowns has its benefits. Especially with respect to when people-centric phenomena will manifest. Knowing ahead of time that people will inject eccentricities, and approximately when, is useful knowledge. The specific details may not be known in advance, but with people being people, people-centric phenomena will manifest. With this knowledge in hand, it is possible to plan accordingly.

This chapter is about seeing into the future. Not literally. Instead, it is about the ability to inspect the predictable chain of events representing the project. Then using this prescience to anticipate in advance actions required and when. This is an opportunity as advantageous as *Credibility* in reducing project execution friction.

THE EVENT HORIZON

A project manager's and contributor's future-looking time abilities will be important to anticipating project requirements. Taking time to regularly look ahead supports small changes in the now. These efforts prevent large corrective actions from being needed in the future. This is interrelated with the concept of *The Things You Don't Know You Don't Know*.

Humans are limited in comprehending or considering a limited amount of time looking forward. This people-centric phenomenon is referred to here as *The Event Horizon*. Everyone's individual forward-looking time threshold is different. Success in project management will require understanding your personal capability in this space as well as that of the contributor's.

A new project is starting with work performed at the customer site. On day one, two colleagues arrive to inspect the work site. Waiting for them are seven pallets stacked with components to install with a project scoped at two weeks to completion. One of the workers was new, and the amount of work expected for just the two of them to deliver, in only two weeks, was causing him anxiety. He shared his concerns with the more experienced co-worker, who confirmed that the project was correctly scoped for on-time completion. The project size and duration were considered reasonable. This is an example of two people confronted with the exact same project situation yet having two very different reactions. Their respective event horizons generated different perceptions when presented with the same workload.

This concept of an event horizon is important to project management. Human beings have limits when it comes to future planning. The observation shared here is that an individual's event horizon in planning over time is based on individual characteristics, experience, and personality. This is not a lifetime constant, though. Experience, the use of project-tracking tools, or even a notebook can improve on the individual's inherent event horizon talent.

A project manager must be able to comprehend the time frame of project execution. If a project is being managed by someone whose personal time horizon is shorter than the project/task they are managing, their stewardship of the project will be less than optimal. The inability to comprehend project execution completely until completion increases project friction.

Similarly, when the number of projects exceeds a person's ability to track them, project needs may not be met. Bandwidth and energy have limits. Project deliverables cannot be optimized or may be missed if they are not properly tracked. Project managers and contributors experience this overload condition as anxiety and stress.

The Event Horizon concept applies to contributors as well. When task execution over time spans beyond an individual contributor's event horizon, it injects friction into project execution. If a contributor is the sole source of needed skills but the time frame is causing problems, try breaking up the project into pieces. These short-duration tasks can then be linked together at a later date.

Requiring an individual to operate significantly outside their event horizon sets them up for failure. Trying to force a fit with a contributor with regard to the event horizon will not be constructive. The project will not benefit, and your relationship with the contributor may suffer. Worst-case scenario: the contributor gets broken by an ask far outside their ability.

An observed sub-phenomenon of *The Event Horizon* is how workload impacts this time sense. Increasing levels of tasking will eventually reach a tipping point. Above that threshold, adding to the workload will decrease an individual's event horizon. This can have unintended consequences. Previously scoped work will be more difficult to manage. The perceived competence of the project manager may be negatively impacted. Project execution may be less skillful than typically enjoyed by the greater organization.

The Event Horizon concept applies to both the project manager and contributors. Awareness is the first step in developing the skills to address this phenomenon's impact on project success. Taking into account individual time-frame capabilities will improve project performance.

THE FUN VERSUS THE UNFUN AND THE EVENT HORIZON

A contributor has been enthusiastically working on their part of a larger project. With every update meeting, progress is being demonstrated. The work is exciting and engaging. Then, not more than a few weeks before project completion, the progress reports change dramatically, no longer showing much in the way of progress.

The project manager asks questions and makes inquiries through their network (*Balls in a Tube*). What has changed? Why has progress slowed to a crawl just as the project nears completion? What the project manager learns is frustrating. The contributor's focus has shifted to another project. However, with closer inspection, it is determined this is not a *The 98% Problem*.

A direct conversation reveals the ugly truth: attention shifted based on interest in the task. The less interesting task was traded for a shiny new one. (*The Shiny Object Distraction, N-1/Matrix*)

Everyone wants to work on fun and interesting things at work. This can help drive better contributor performance if the project is the shiny new awesomeness everyone wants to work on. When people find time to work on the fun, productivity soars. Unfortunately, what is left behind is the nearly complete project.

This phenomenon is the dark side to combining a matrix organization with an uninteresting or undesirable project. Once the fun has been squeezed from the opportunity, a matrix contributor has the flexibility to push the ball out of the tube and focus elsewhere.

Acknowledgment of this phenomenon provides the opportunity to strategize for this challenging situation. When an opportunity to work on something more interesting than the current effort presents itself, prevention of a loss of focus can be anticipated and prevented.

CONSTRUCTIVE PERSISTENCE

$$1.00^{365} = 1$$

$$1.01^{365} = 37.8$$

Once upon a time, there was a calibration technician at a contract electronics manufacturer. One of the customers transferred all their test equipment as part of the subcontracting. One particular dilapidated piece of test equipment required attention from one of the customer's engineers on a regular basis. This equipment became non-functional at an inconvenient time. The customer's engineer worked all day trying to get it restarted. And then the next day. Four full workdays were spent troubleshooting. He worked through and eliminated each possible failure point, calmly executing his plan to root out the cause of the problem. This encounter serves as an inspiration of professional persistence personified.

> Persistence: Firm or obstinate continuance in a course of action in spite of difficulty or opposition.

Persistence is repeated efforts over time in pursuit of a goal, and persistence is necessary to accomplish challenging tasks. Constructive persistence is a skilled approach required for successful project management efforts. An observed phenomenon with persistence is the lack of understanding regarding the constructive part. Without a plan for the constructive component, interactions of an iterative nature become a source of frustration, manifesting unconstructive behavior such as bullying and manipulation.

A task required of a project manager is repeatedly following up on project details. Contributor communications not received when expected will need to be solicited so the loop can be closed on project tasks. To track down these details, a project manager needs persistence tempered with a polite and professional approach.

> Just hammering away for an update will likely not generate the desired short-term results nor support a constructive long-term relationship with the target of this approach.

When it is necessary to repeatedly approach someone to get a response, it helps to vary the method of the ask. Change up the communications channel: email one time, voice the next. Try to weave the ask into other interactions. Change the structure and language of the ask. Use a positive tone. No one responds well to a monotone, semi-confrontational request. These methods plant the ask in the contributor's mind. Wait perhaps two or more weeks and reapproach. "Remember that thing we talked about a few weeks ago? I went back and looked at it again, and the value is still there. We can still move forward. What do you think?" Since you gave them the time to let their subconscious work through it, it may bring them to see the opportunity. Others may know the how or why human psychology manifests this peculiarity, but the *Constructive Persistence* works more often than not.

An aspect of this phenomenon is people having a reset time after declining something. In video game terms, this is a cooldown. If the ask is repeated too soon after the most recent declined ask, without sufficient cooldown, the outcome will be unchanged and the undesirable response previously received is reinforced. The duration of this delay time is unique to the individual and the complexity of the request.

Remember, persistence and antagonism are not the same thing. Don't be antagonistic. Make notes of all the little details that need to be followed up. If a response is taking too long, make that call (*In Person for Maximum Effect*). Remain polite and professional. Be a coach and advocate (*Be Positive*). Provide guidance and offer support, but keep pushing for results.

When asked, sometimes a potential project contributor says no. Sometimes they say hell no. Sometimes they tell you to go to hell. It can get rough. Stay calm and professional. Do not burn bridges. This is just round one of what may be a long engagement. Stay focused on the final goal and not on the negativity being shared. After the initial refusal, give the contributor time and space while you work on your plan B. Then go back for round two. Review your message and approach. Look for details that will resonate better with whom you are trying to influence. Enlist allies. Ask for insight from mentors. Stay calm and professional. Sometimes round two fails. Start planning round three. This is an endurance and communications game. Never give up, but give the person you're trying to persuade space and time. This is important: Do not wear out your welcome. The rookie mistake is to keep pounding away. That is counterproductive. The goal is to let the proposal percolate in their subconscious.

A consistent, professionally and politely delivered constructively persistent approach establishes project execution ground rules. Contributors will have awareness of expectations and engage accordingly. A varied and skilled, people-centric approach to persistence delivers results.

Bounded Speculative Paranoia

> Only the paranoid survive.

An individual was having problems sleeping when the television was on, and not just in the room with the sleeping person but anywhere in the house. Turning the volume down did not resolve the issue. The television being on was the problem, not how loud it was.

This situation occurred before flat-screen TV's when TV's used CRT's (cathode ray tubes). The image on the screen was created by sweeping a beam of electrons across the back of the screen really fast. That sweep frequency was 20,000 cycles per second (20 kHz). There is likely an engineering reasons for why 20kHz was chosen, perhaps because it is the lowest frequency above the human hearing range that created quality images. Yes, human hearing range. Turns out, *most* people cannot hear such a high frequency. But *some* people can, and

20kHz cuts through the walls like any high-frequency noise would be expected to.

The individual affected knew there was a problem with the television being on. The rest of the people involved did not see a problem. How is such an obscure problem resolved? With a healthy dose of *Bounded speculative paranoia*. Eventually the person affected graduated as an electrical engineer and realized what the problem was. He could hear 20 kHz and could not sleep. His roommates could not hear it and thought he was crazy.

Project management is an endeavor that rewards those who plan ahead. The opportunities for strategic thinking and reasonable contingency planning delivering value are practically infinite. Experience with complex projects imbues a skill for analyzing the project and the people involved. The goal is to find where it can all go wrong and prepare contingencies accordingly. Bounded speculative paranoia will drive looking for the potential weak links in the critical path. Where can things go wrong? What actions can be taken ahead of time to reduce the risk of that happening? Is there a backup plan ready to go? This is a probability game of how likely it is that bad things will happen and what contingencies need to be in place to compensate. It's risk management taking into account factors learned from experience and critical thinking focused on the reasonably possible.

Aspects of the project demonstrating, *The Free-Association Apocalypse* or *Unnatural Conversation* characteristics benefit from some *Bounded speculative paranoia* attention. The injection of explaining why things won't work or the absence of delivered value helps shut down unconstructive lines of discussion.

Speculative paranoia is an expert-level project management skill. It helps address several other people-centric phenomena and is an important tool in the toolbox. Developing this skill takes time and self-review. Input from others on your approach is required to keep the efforts within rational bounds. After all, it is not called paranoia for nothing.

This is not my first rodeo

As projects increase in size, complexity, duration, and technical requirements, so does the need for increasingly skilled and talented project management. In addition to skills, experience brings understanding of how projects execute. A seasoned veteran will remain unflappable while the project inferno rages and the collective effort is threatened. A project manager's experience delivers a singular characteristic to the effort: calmness. Project execution, deadlines, and challenges will generate anxiety and other unconstructive emotions in participants. Undamped, they can begin to resonate and affect performance. A calm hand on the wheel really helps in these situations.

Since everyone has to start somewhere and the needed experience comes from, well, experience, consider adding a little stoicism to your project management demeanor. Be (or fake being) a calm, even-tempered person providing the rock that others need during the never-ending challenges of project execution.

This phenomenon of experience is both obvious and misunderstood. The idea that experience delivers value is a commonly held belief. *How* it delivers that value is often not obvious. The need for even-tempered project management is worth exploring.

The things you know you know

There are things you know you know. Budget, available contributors, project charter . . . these are all straightforward. The project manager knows the foundation for project structure. Defining and considering the aspects known gives the project structure points of reference (*Asking Good Questions, Perform Due Diligence*). It will also reveal aspects of the project requiring further definition. What is known gives confidence while defining the path forward.

Once this concept is acknowledged, experience will lead to an epiphany: realizing there are things you know you don't know . . .

The things you know you don't know

Standard operating procedure—day one: make a list of the unknowns. Often referred to as gaps.

There are things you know you don't know. For example, a vendor's real delivery date. You have the expected date of delivery on the quote, but when it actually will arrive is unknown. Then there are time estimates versus the final outcome. And estimated cost versus final cost. Categorizing these undefined loose ends is a risk analysis. In most cases, awareness is what is needed to react if the unknowns go out of tolerance.

Often, a source of misunderstanding can be identified at the beginning of a project. Start by asking questions probing for the clues (*Asking Good Questions*). The questions have their roots in experience and are targeted at aspects of the project demonstrating attention-getting complexity or vagueness. This type of inspection will reveal project details not likely to support success.

Example:

Step 1: Deliver the proposal.

Step 2: Organize the team.

Step 3: Something magical happens here.

Word to the wise: That step 3 warrants further investigation.

Bounded Speculative Paranoia delivers value in this space. This is a gap where turn-the-crank-style project management is challenged.

THE THINGS YOU DON'T KNOW YOU DON'T KNOW

Engineering minus sales equals scrap.

Anything that can go wrong, will go wrong. And at the worst possible moment. –
Murphy's Law

No book on project management is complete without a reference to Murphy's Law. It's as immutable and constant as gravity and the speed of light. Twelve words representing the purest truth.

A long time ago, in a land far, far away, there were two warring kings. With the kings evenly matched, their war was without end. Both sides could bring the same number of archers and knights to the field. The kings were at a stalemate.

One day, a salesman came to the gate seeking an audience with one of the kings. He was ushered into the throne room to make his pitch. Before the salesman could speak, the king bellowed, "I hate salespeople, and I am far too busy for this. Begone!"

The salesman graciously bowed, thanked the king for his time, and left. He traveled to the opposing king's castle. After knocking and explaining his purpose, the salesman was marched into the throne room and his presence was announced.

This king glared down from his throne and said, "I hate salespeople, and I am very busy. You have five minutes."

The salesman bowed and began his presentation. "Thank you for your time, Your Majesty. My presentation will be short. The opportunity I bring to you today is a new invention ... the machine gun."

This is an excellent example of a disruptive technology being introduced and learning about something you didn't know you didn't know.

Spending a few minutes to think about and inspect those things you don't know you don't know can positively impact your project. With enough project management experience, this concept will be felt at the core of your being. Is a critical piece of test equipment due for calibration right when testing is planned? Is a key subject-matter expert retiring in the middle of the project timeline? It is likely no one has considered this or would think to volunteer this information.

There will be things negatively impacting project execution that cannot be planned for. However, with experience (and a little *Bounded Speculative Paranoia*), risk mitigation in this area is possible.

WHAT ARE EXPERTS GOOD FOR?

Bob had worked at this nuclear power plant since it was built. Every year, during the month of July, Bob would take a box fan down to the generator room, open the door, and position the fan to blow air in. This would, in Bob's opinion, prevent moisture buildup. His concern was that condensation could create an unsafe condition. Then one day Bob retired, and July rolled around. Nobody propped open the door with a box fan. Humidity built up, and BOOM! Something very expensive shorted out and catastrophically failed. Now the generator room has a fancy dehumidifier built in.

There are experts like Bob who know the secrets. Your task as a project manager is not to become the expert that Bob is. Instead, become an expert at finding Bob, whoever and wherever he/she is. Subject-matter experts know things. They can do things, and they have done things in the past.

> Subject-matter experts know things. *They can do things.* And they have done things in the past.

When a project's existing pool of talent is the gap preventing progress, resolution requires expert input. There is a need to include others as project contributors or to bring your questions to someone who has the needed expertise.

Subject-matter experts are experienced colleagues focused on a particular area. They represent a source of knowledge that project managers will be going back to over and over. This may have to be done as the project is executing (*In-Flight Missile Repairman*) to prevent the gap from speed-bumping the project. *Asking Good Questions, In Person for Maximum Effect,* and *Credibility* will play important roles here. The communication challenges experienced in these engagements can be especially taxing (*Smart People Think Complicated Is Fun*). *Unnatural Conversation* can rear its ugly head. Be ready to gently, with tact, guide the discussion back to the task at hand.

Subject-matter experts are typically enthusiastic about providing their unique support. There are exceptions, but people this experienced as to be considered subject-matter experts are not threatened by sharing their knowledge. They are also very enthusiastic about the subject in which they are experts. That is why they became an expert. That enthusiasm drives them to want to share. That's a positive trait to leverage. For many subject-matter experts, their contribution is a demonstration of skill and value to the organization. It is an affirmation of their usefulness. Being the only person who can make something happen is a nice ego boost. Oddly enough, subject-matter experts rarely demonstrate the challenges associated with *Insufficient Gravitas*. Apparently, when an individual has real talent, deep skill, and knowledge, concerns about associating with "less-important" people are not an issue.

Word to the wise: Experts are often senior members of the organization and well-connected (*Insinuation and Gossip are Verboten*). In addition to providing expertise, there is likely a fantastic networking opportunity.

There is value in letting subject-matter experts ramble (*Run Silent, Run Deep*). They often know more than they know they know. By paying close attention, important information will be shared.

Constructive professional relationships with subject-matter experts are a necessity. Develop those subject-matter experts' engagement skills.

HOW WE DID IT IN THE GOOD OLD DAYS: TOXIC NOSTALGIA

The phenomenon here is when experienced contributors steer project goals based on past performance. Identifying obsolete approaches that creep into a project due to contributor nostalgia and comfort level is a skill. Maneuvering these unconstructive influences back out of the project (*Immovable Object, Change Management*) is the needed complementary skill. Do not let *How We did It in the Good Old Days* set the path forward. Experienced, long-standing employees are valued contributors. The goal is to leverage their skills and experience while maintaining a fresh perspective. Experienced colleagues sharing past outcomes is a good thing (*What Are Experts Good For?*). Institutional knowledge is valuable (*The things you know you know*). Use reminiscing about events and *Asking Good Questions* to build a more robust project.

These are challenging engagements. The colleagues pushing nostalgia are often more experienced, have been with the company longer than the project manager, and, in many cases are subject-matter experts on the topic. Successfully preventing *How We did It in the Good Old Days* from infecting a project is an expert engagement. A project manager needs a robust portfolio of project management tools in their toolbox to be successful in this space.

OUT OF PHASE

A writer has a wholistic view of creating a book, which has stages of activity. The rough draft comes before beta review and multiple polishing reads. Then the professional edit is followed by the final review. If the rough draft is shared with someone for a critical review, the writer is likely looking for commentary on characters, story, and flow. What they may receive is a critique of grammar, sentence structure, and punctuation. The requestor and the reviewer did not engage at the same phase of the project. They did not communicate properly; thus efforts focused on different stages of the effort, and, as a result, no useful work was delivered.

The *Out of Phase* phenomenon occurs when two people are approaching the situation from different phases in the project. If the project manager is preparing for a task others assume is already complete, all kinds of misunderstandings occur. It's important to be aware of where others are in the project process and to keep ongoing activities aligned.

Surviving mistakes

Accelerated learning through failure!

Human beings are not accuracy machines. The error rate of humans while engaged in repetitive tasks or when making decisions is disturbingly high. A case could be made that we probably should not be allowed to do these types of things. But, since nothing will get done if humans do not do it, we will just have to make do.

> A guy worked in a factory. He had a good attitude, always showed up on time, took instruction well, and worked hard. Two weeks into the job, he hurt himself using the drill press. This injury resulted in a trip to the emergency room. A few weeks later he cut through the power cord of the saw he was sawing with. Not long after that, he had another accident. He was let go. His supervisor said the guy was a good employee except he was accident-prone. You can't train that out of someone, and they can't stay in the factory because of it. He had to let him go.

Sometimes an error rate is so high it forces action. Sometimes making mistakes can have an upside. The learning curve from mistakes is steep, but if you learn from your mistakes, you can reap long-term benefits. Being prepared for mistakes (by you or others) is prudent. A little *Bounded Speculative Paranoia* helps in this space.

Conclusion

This chapter shared several observed phenomena and ideas for addressing them. Many of which manifest in subtle and remarkably irritating ways. Phenomena regarding time frame, expert engagement, and risk and failure management are typically higher-skill-level engagements. The return on investment in these spaces is exceptional once the basics are mastered.

11

PEOPLE BEING PEOPLE

There are project management phenomena linked to the inner psychology, personality, and life experiences of the people involved. For the purposes of project management, these characteristics cannot be changed, only compensated for. The only approaches are engagement, work-around, acknowledgment, and compensation strategies.

> It is difficult to get a person to understand something when their salary depends on their not understanding.

In the case of unconstructive behavior, this is an opportunity to develop people-management skills. This chapter is about people being people and how to prevent unconstructive, people-centric project management phenomena from impacting project execution.

Behavior Phenomena

There are personality traits that can improve project performance or require acknowledgment and skill to engage constructively and navigate to success.

For example, there are the contrarians. Engaging them through discussion of solutions and progress is a good approach. Asking for more clarification about their objections can mitigate the opposition. Contrarianism is a reflex reaction and not typically a well-thought-out objection.

Then there is the asker of impertinent questions. Under the guise of attempting to add value to the discussion, they will deliver inflammatory questions that are only tangentially relevant. The tangential part is the weakness. If the question is not directly relevant, request clarification of the path forward. This will reveal the irrelevance of the question.

The above are generalizations of common challenges. What follows below are specific people-being-people phenomena.

ONLY IDEAL SOLUTIONS NEED APPLY

This phenomenon is project elements being made ultra-important that were never important before. The previous version was never reviewed, but this new one gets a super deep, ultra-detailed inspection. Opening the project to change can enable an only-ideal-solutions-will-be-accepted condition. The fact that the prior project structure was not perfect is irrelevant to those demanding perfection. This is a *The Crap/Perfection Juxtaposition* phenomenon only from a different angle. The proposition for an unachievable, ideal solution will be shared as the only path forward. Only after significant effort and no small amount of time has passed will there be a relenting in this approach.

Only Ideal Solutions Need Apply is also a variant on *The Free-Association Apocalypse*. A project is being reconsidered, and this allows the negative phenomena previously filtered out to reemerge.

Don't let the same phenomenon that was a challenge before wreak havoc a second time.

SANDBAG CONTRIBUTORS

There are contributors who are not invested in the project moving forward. They may not be interested in the project, or they may have other, more stimulating opportunities. It may even be a case of "not my idea" or even jealousy. Regardless, it is important to identify sandbag contributors early.

Signs that sandbagging is occurring includes a lack of enthusiasm, passive-aggressive questions, recalling similar failed projects, and endless requests for clarification. A *Muddy the Water* and *The Circular Firing Squad* experience that never ends. Demanding perfection or impossible delivery deadlines is another way to sandbag a project. *Hooking On* can also be leveraged to crush a project. Be aware of potential sandbagging, especially when project scope demands are strangely unconstructive. Most of the sandbagging approaches are variations of phenomena shared in this book. Find them and construct a path forwards.

THE LIGHT-BULB ELECTRICIAN

A lightning storm the night before had knocked out half the electric motors in a manufacturing facility. Over the next two days, the maintenance team worked long hours to get everything running again.

As failed motors were swapped out, the plant engineer learned there was an arrangement for a local company to rebuild the motors and upgrade them to improve reliability. It was explained that the motors were upgraded to "H" rated windings to improve lifespan in the hot factory environment. The arrangement was odd, and the explanation did not make sense. Another motor supplier was solicited looking for clarification of "H" windings. Their salesperson came on-site and made a no-nonsense presentation on industrial electric motor technology. It turned out all these motors already came with "H" windings from the manufacturer. After making the change to a more reputable motor supplier, the next lightning storm only knocked out one or two motors.

Despite claiming deep expertise, the factory electrician had never disputed the motor supplier's claims. His technical knowledge was insufficient to prevent this corrupt arrangement from occurring.

On occasion, during the search for contributors with specialized skills, self-proclaimed experts will be encountered who are not really experts. These are the so-called light-bulb electricians because they only know how to change light bulbs. They survive by virtue of work history and providing their underwhelming expertise to people who do not know any better.

If an example is sought of what a know-nothing subject-matter expert sounds like, just look up "retro-encabulator" on the internet.

From a project management standpoint, this is a challenge. The low-capability subject-matter expert may be the only contributor available for aspects of the project. What to do? Minimize the impact of their incompetence on the project (*Perform Due Diligence, Allies*). Scrutinize their every input (*Ask Good Questions*). Don't confront them about their incompetence. If they have survived this long, they likely have friends in high places—or their longevity gives them a credibility the project manager does not have. Be polite, be professional. Many of these people have egos starkly out of proportion to their level of competence. Recognizing the situation early on and planning the limits of their involvement will protect the project's path; it will also minimize negative outcomes related to incompetence-inspired missteps by a mislabeled subject-matter expert (*The Long Game*).

THE INVERSE COMPETENCY VERSUS LIKEABILITY MAXIM

There are subject matter experts who appear to short their social engagement skills for increased competency in their chosen profession. Resembling a video game min-maxing strategy, this can result in critical contributors who are unique collaboration experiences. This leads to the strange and uncomfortable situation where the curmudgeon expresses themselves in unconstructive ways and the project manager will just have to accept it. Correct, the contributor's input is required, and they are likely a valued colleague. In some cases, the level of abrasiveness is unprofessional. Regardless, the project manager's responses must remain professional.

This phenomenon requires dedication and skill while navigating the situation. The goal is to deliver the project, not fix people.

FULL KAMIKAZE: THE TENSION HAMMER

There is a point when persistence transitions from constructive to bullying. As a project manager, this will be a common experience.

Example: An aspect of the project is now frozen with no changes allowed. A colleague wants to make a change. Even after a detailed explanation of the frozen situation, the discussion is not resolved, and he continues pushing. It becomes obvious that he plans on coming at the project manager over and over until he gets his way.

> Are you done yet? Are you done yet? Are you done yet?

He is going *Full Kamikaze* and taking persistence to a level that is no longer professional. It is transitioning to bullying. Where is this line crossed? One possible interpretation is between attempts three and four. Anyone wanting change gets three tries, and after that, it should end. Getting three attempts has some sort of special meaning to humans. If people are given the opportunity to attempt something three times, they are generally satisfied that everything that can be done has been done. With the fourth attempt, there is a problem. Time is now being wasted. Three times declined should be the professional limit. Unless management is now weighing in, the discussion is over. Tell them the decision has been made. Hang up on them if necessary, because apparently, they cannot get the hint.

One variant of *Full Kamikaze* is a peer calling someone out in front of colleagues by assigning a task publicly, in front of the team, verbally or by email. *This task is important; the team will expect your completion of this by Wednesday*. This is pinning a task to a person without getting their feedback first. By calling someone out publicly, a name associated with a task, and a completion date, most will see it as a done deal. There is social pressure because other participants see this as a way to avoid their being assigned the same task. It also leverages that the ones assigned the task are not likely to push back in the high-visibility way this situation requires.

Another variant of the kamikaze approach is to "shake the cage." This is an aggressive variant that will include leadership in copy as the *Full Kamikaze* plays out. Insinuation will be woven into the messaging, and the overall effect is that of threatening.

Why do people go *Full Kamikaze*? Because it works. This form of bullying is quite successful. Just hammer the source until they give you what you want so you go away. Just as in the unfair and derogatory saying "Those who cannot do, teach. Those who cannot teach, administrate." Those who cannot develop effective communication, credibility, or leadership skills can always bully.

> Those who cannot develop effective communication, credibility, or leadership skills can always bully.

For many, *Full Kamikaze* is sourced in frustration and trying to find a way to achieve forward motion. The perpetrator finally arrives at a state of mind where they just hammer at the thing they want to move. They are maxing out the tension to hammer the focus where they think it should be.

Constructive Persistence and *Full Kamikaze* occupy different places on the persuasion spectrum. One is a professional approach this book advocates for. The other will eventually push contributors subject to it on a regular basis to engage in avoidance.

I KNOW WHAT I AM DOING

This is the phenomenon when an experienced person will take control and direct everyone's actions with grating specificity until the task is complete. The situation requires skill and experience in the driver's seat or there is a learning opportunity that requires step-by-step direction. Regardless, there are no debates, no group consensus. Just a declaration of who is in charge and to follow instructions.

> Sometimes it is necessary for someone to be appointed overlord.

The most constructive approach is to treat these situations as a learning opportunity. If the leadership is appointing someone as the project or process overlord, there might be a reason.

THEY ARE A PEACH

There are individuals who are of exceptional abrasiveness. Grumpy, a little angry, blunt, and plain-speaking, they are often inflammatory in their approach to communication. It is often the case that such individuals are competent and make good project contributors (*The Inverse Competency Versus Likeability Maxim*). Their abrasiveness will tone down over time after the initial introduction. It helps to have a thick skin and to not react to their social impropriety.

Then there are those who complain incessantly to get what they want. Why? Because it works. Like going *Full Kamikaze*, this is a form of bullying. Complaining is annoying, and most people will give the complainer what they want just to make the complaining stop. Working with a variety of contributors will inevitably lead to engaging with unpleasant people. Regardless, getting along with them is not optional.

There is a rare version of the peach phenomenon termed here "the rotten peach." A peach taking every interaction to maximum unpleasantness. These negative experiences are likely an indication of a bigger problem.

A rotten peach uses unfriendliness to cover incompetence, driving people away to prevent visibility of poorly delivered outcomes. Some people are just unpleasant.

Name-droppers

Name-droppers are a special breed of challenging to work with. They see themselves as very important, and as important people, they only work with other important people. Narcissists who like to drop names during meetings often do so as a way to intimidate or influence. There can be an element of the ridiculous as the names dropped go up higher and higher in the organization.

What to do? Ignore their unconstructive behavior. The people represented by the dropped names are not likely to have any exposure to the project. If it makes a contributor feel better to name-drop, good for them. It should have no effect on actions taken, though.

Name-droppers are often ambitious with a high sense of self-worth and socially consciousness. It bothers them to see others deliver up new ideas or success. Remarkable resistance will be introduced by these types if they see a concept eclipsing what they have shared. It is an unconstructive competitive instinct.

Ignore or work around *Name-droppers*.

But they are yelling at me

Sometimes people yell. Perhaps not as much in today's work environment, but some still work in male-dominated, old-school industries where old-fashioned dressing down is still practiced.

Handling these unprofessional situations and personalities is part of the project manager experience. Stay calm. Do not get angry back. Develop a staying-cool response. This is a difficult skill to master. Especially if the yeller is a top-of-the-line problem. But stay calm. Listen to their words. Likely, they are yelling because their boss yelled at them, or the situation is just too frustrating. Let them get whatever is bothering them out of their system. Then calmly address their concerns.

Here is the weird part. By not starting a fight in response to their venting, you will become closer with that person. After remaining professional and not reacting to the histrionics, this somehow builds credibility and demonstrates you are a good-faith partner who will stick with them no matter what.

The first time trying this tactic is a leap of faith. If everything goes well, what happens on the other side may surprise you.

CHICKEN LITTLE SYNDROME

There is a children's story where the main character, Chicken Little, runs around in public telling everyone the sky is falling. Chicken Little's histrionic outburst proclaiming an apocalyptic event is nigh is untrue.

Project management has a phenomenon that is similar. There are individuals who are part of a project or adjacent to the project who will feel the need to make a pronouncement of failure. They will not consult with anyone to confirm that what they perceive as a problem actually is a problem. Instead, during a meeting, they will tell everyone some aspect of the project is incorrect and that some or all of the project will fail. These individuals will not have spoken to anyone regarding messaging or what is the best way to present this. They will also not have met with the project manager to discuss (*The Pre-Meeting Meeting*). Due diligence is not part of a *Chicken Little Syndrome* experience. Perpetrators of this phenomenon will often share their misbegotten inflammatory interpretation of the situation with anyone who will listen. This includes senior or even executive leadership. The project manager will have to address the situation and communicate that what is being said is untrue.

People who deliver this type of unconstructive message are typically serial perpetrators. *Chicken Little Syndrome* can manifest beyond the occasional individual. Some organizations have this baked into their culture. A sort of passive-aggressive sport.

A project manager will need to set ground rules with contributors about who delivers project messaging to leadership.

THE SHINY-OBJECT DISTRACTION: SHIFTING FOCUS

Contributor autonomy in the matrix environment and N-1 work overload create susceptibility to distraction. The N-1 work overload enables a subconscious desire for something fun or new. This phenomenon disrupts organized project execution (*Balls in a Tube*). It also negatively impacts project execution velocity in the N-1 matrix space.

What are the types of distractions? Contributors who need a mental health diversion. Other project managers who show up with that new cool thing to work on. Managers who ask for that "one, easy quick thing."

When encountering this phenomenon, keep in mind that explicitly calling out a contributor's loss of focus is bad form. Contributors demonstrating this behavior will not appreciate the public shaming. Often, they do not even realize the behavior is happening.

There is a synergy to be found between the *Shiny-Object Distraction* and *Distraction Elimination* concepts. Aggressively delivering *Distraction Elimination* dramatically reduces the potential for a *Shiny-Object Distraction* event.

SHORT-DOG SYNDROME

Many experience the *Short-Dog Syndrome* phenomenon while in the military. People who are grouped together for tasks will keep their focus until close to the end of the task's time. It also comes up when people are retiring or have resigned but will still be around for the obligatory time period. Perhaps this is the root cause of *The 98% Problem* or an artifact of *The Event Horizon*. Once the end of their association is close (two weeks seems to be the most common time frame), social cohesion breaks down.

The closer the exit date, the less focused people become. In addition to being less helpful or responsive, belligerence may rear its ugly head. There is a perceived opportunity to air past grievances without fear of repercussion. Most people are not aware they are exhibiting this behavior.

Knowing this phenomenon is going to happen takes most of the stress out of it. Get what you need before hitting those two weeks. Be ready for some unorthodox behavior. When you aren't surprised by it, this phenomenon is manageable.

LOSING THAT NEW CAR SMELL

When you are new to an organization, everyone wants to meet you. When engaging with colleagues on your first assignments, every request is supported and every question answered. Then, several months later, the responsiveness drops precipitously. There is a honeymoon period where everyone supports the new person. The length of this time varies from organization to organization. Your professionalism and likeability will extend or shorten this time.

What to do about this phenomenon? Don't be a burden (*Asking Good Questions*). Be polite (*Say Thank You*). Take advantage of the increased engagement to build bridges and meet people (*In Person for Maximum Effect*). Learn as much as possible. Awareness that the good times will soon come to an end helps. Plan for the transition. Leverage the temporary high engagement for future success.

STOP TOUCHING THINGS! - ENDLESS CHANGES

There are things that should be left alone until it is understood why they are the way they are. Look up Chesterton's Fence on the internet for some philosophical guidance on this phenomenon. Don't touch things you do not have a complete understanding of (*Things You Don't Know You Don't Know*). This includes both project and process. Don't confuse your intellect, skills, experience, position in the hierarchy, and education as a license to do anything you wish.

There was a company that manufactured a machine that used a cooling tower. This is a tall tank of water with a pump at the top. The pump sucks water from the bottom of the tank, some seven meters below.

One day, the plumber installing one of these cooling towers called the manufacturer to ask where the one-way check valve is. This gadget keeps the water from running out of the pipe when the pump is not running. The one-way check valve is a standard bit of the install kit.

The manufacturing supervisor was asked, and he responded with a shrug. It didn't make sense why it was not included. He checked the bill of materials and found there was no longer a check valve included with the piping kit. This explained why it was missing. The paperwork did not require it. But why was it missing from the bill of materials now? The engineering manager was brought in. He was also mystified and checked the engineering drawings. The check valve was found to be missing from the drawings. The engineering manager pulled the engineering change requests and found that the CEO had made the change to the bill of materials and not consulted anyone.

The pump had a check valve built into it. On the schematic of the piping, this check valve looked the same as the one down inside the tank. To save money, since they are obviously the same thing (the piping schematic says so!), the CEO made the change, believing it would save money. No one else was consulted.

The lesson here is not to touch things that are not part of your core competency without consulting others. Making changes in such a way disturbs the project focus. Don't do this. Know your limitations and develop a technique for reaching out to others on unfamiliar topics.

Personality

INTJ death glare—characteristic INTJ
facial expression

The Myers-Briggs Type Indicator (MBTI) can provide guidance on personality characteristics. There are those whose event horizon and capacity for strategy are excellent (INTJ). Others are a natural for people to look to for leadership (ENTJ). There are personalities that are born cheerleaders. Some have a predilection for communicating and connecting with others (extroverts). Leaders who can read people (ENTP).

Most children's cartoon villains are based
on the INTJ personality type. Children are
taught to hate and fear INTJ's from
infancy.

As a project manager, awareness of the strengths and opportunities for improvement derived from personality are worth exploring. The goal here is not a Machiavellian power trip. Consideration of a colleague's common humanity contributes to a positive work experience. It also delivers opportunities for synergies and the corresponding productivity improvements. A true win-win for everyone.

Learning about personality and developing the skill to evaluate those you engage with every day can only bring you success.

THE IMMUNE RESPONSE TO TAKING INSTRUCTION

Can you take instruction? To not object and do what you're told? It's a skill to be able to set aside your ego and questions and just follow instructions. This skill is taught in the military but is not well understood outside that experience. People do not like being told what to do. The natural response is to ask, "Why?"

There are times when a contributor's understanding is not unnecessary. Perhaps there is not enough time for the explanation. Or the information needed for a complete explanation is confidential. Then there are those situations where a contributor's understanding of what is being asked would influence their actions. Sometimes your supervisor's patience is running low, and they would appreciate someone just doing what they are told for once without questioning it.

Project management has opportunities to give and to receive instruction. Understanding your own abilities in this space is important. Sensitivity to others' limitations in taking instruction is equally important. Just because you see the value in this topic does not mean others do. There is a shortage of people who can take instruction. A seasoned manager will recognize and value these few executors who can.

MUDDY THE WATER: ANTI-FOCUS

There are communications where one of the parties involved is not interested in resolving or clarifying anything. Every input from them, every comment, every point of contribution is tangential. They throw out straw man arguments left and right. They point to failed past efforts.

Tenuous connections are drawn to other products, services, people, or even other companies. They reply to questions with their own questions, often not related to the topic being discussed. They talk about what is being discussed at length while adding nothing to the path forward.

Muddy the Water contributors must be isolated, and their contribution highlighted for what it is: unconstructive. Once identified, work to minimize the offending contributor's project exposure. Communications with such people must be overly specific.

This is not always a sandbagging event. Some people are unfocused and unable to spiral into a coherent message. This *Muddy the Water* person may or may not know what they are doing. Don't call them out, as this will be viewed as inflammatory. Just keep isolating and clarifying. Other colleagues are likely aware of the situation. Knowledge of this phenomenon and limiting the spread is the goal here.

PRIMA DONNAS

There are those within an organization that have a high opinion of themselves. They are not humble. Perhaps they are high performers or long-term deliverers of value to the company. Or they may just be arrogant jerks. If the arrogance does not interfere with the project, there is no reason to interfere with their fantasy. The good news: people exhibiting these behaviors typically lack the depth and humility to develop real skills and therefore are not likely to be needed as project contributors. Look past the personality and focus on the project.

JIGGLING THE HANDLE: UNNECESSARY COMPLEXITY

Jiggling the Handle is a variation on the *Smart People Think Complicated is Fun* phenomenon. This phenomenon manifests in both products and processes. They are often created as an artifact of *The 98% Problem* and actualize as irritating and obscure interactive features. If there is any level of complexity involved, expect *Jiggling the Handle* to manifest.

A customer is using a product. Its performance is not as advertised. They contact the manufacturer. The solution is an undocumented setting impossible to find without the subject-matter expert explaining. This is called the *Jiggling the Handle* fix. People "in the know" just make the change. Flip a hidden switch. Slap the side of the machine. Cycle power. Sacrifice a chicken. Whatever. Anyone else watching the undocumented, non-intuitive effort required is disturbed by it and shakes their head. *Who thought this was a good idea?*

Processes can have similar struggles, where some aspect is poorly documented and not user-friendly. The work proceeds as intended until a point. Then there is an operation required that is neither intuitive nor even rational. Something was left unfinished, or customer experience was not a factor in the development process. Please keep in mind that the smart people who created this situation do not see complexity the same way.

This is a difficult communications and guidance challenge. Resolving something not seen as a negative without inadvertently insulting people who may be proud of the technological terror they have created. Jiggling the handle configurations can snowball as technical debt builds up until almost no one can figure it out. These cascading, overlapping multiple interactions are best avoided. Remove *Jiggling the Handle* characteristics from your projects as quickly as possible. Once you are aware this phenomenon is common, instances of its existence become all too easy to spot.

TECHNICAL CORRECTNESS: CORRECT IMPLEMENTATION

When a technical product fails to deliver, the baleful glare of those expecting its release will fall on those involved. This is something that is just understood, whether the project deliverable is not performing as advertised or there was an epic crash and burn.

Technical Correctness is the philosophy is that there is a correct way to accomplish what is being asked. This will be stated with absolute confidence. Other approaches would meet the requirements but are considered less than ideal. Correct implementation prevents flexibility and has elements of *How We did It in the Good Old Days*.

Anchor project efforts in best practices, existing proven tech, or solutions built from previous experience. A well-defined specification will make a significant difference. The more ambiguity, the more perfectionists veer toward ideal solutions and correct implementation.

Remember, perfectionists have an *Only Ideal Designs Need Apply* fixation. If a window of opportunity is presented, they will move the approach to correct implementation. Be prepared ahead of time, ask lots of questions, and keep this concept in mind. There is a difference between what is ideal and what is practically possible. In many ways, this is a variant of *The Crap/Perfection Juxtaposition*.

It should be noted that there is nothing wrong with perfectionists leaning toward correct implementation. This pursuit of excellence combined with adherence to acknowledging real-world impact is important to success. Acknowledging this phenomenon improves the flexibility of solutions when executing a practical delivery.

THE BIGGER HAMMER

If a little is good, a lot must be better. Working harder, not smarter. This sums up *The Bigger Hammer Approach*.

There are elegant, efficient solutions. An enlightened, considered development of project objectives, contributors, and resources through the skilled application of experience and intellect. A path forward that everyone involved will be proud to participate in. Then there is *The Bigger Hammer* phenomenon: too much work or too much overly complicated work for the desired outcome. A fundamental understanding of the task and its execution is missing. In some cases, it is a legacy artifact of *How We did It in the Good Old Days*.

The Bigger Hammer phenomenon is a common outcome of big-picture solutions. Attempting to realize an epic vision without taking into account the details. *Angels on a Pinhead* is a bigger hammer approach. Increasing workload while decreasing output. The conclusion most arrived at: more people are needed, or people need to work longer hours.

Regardless of the source, if the thought coming to mind is, "There must be a better way," then this may be an opportunity to add some innovation and intellect into process improvement.

THE SILVER BULLET IMPROBABILITY

Klaatu Verata Nickto – The one thing that fixes everything.

Frustration may drive people to look for the one thing that fixes everything all at once. Often a novel technical solution will be proposed. Some who picked up this book had the thought to look for the secret to getting things done. To learn, "If I just do this or say that," their projects will start executing flawlessly. Perhaps a checklist or a magic phrase such as "Sprinkle some fairy dust on it" or "Pull a rabbit out of my hat." The phenomenon is the search for the silver bullet to making all their project efforts deliver on time and under budget. That kind of silver-bullet thinking is an impediment to success in and of itself.

Silver bullet seeking can be driven by too many *The Bigger Hammer* experiences, including frustration with tasks and work requirements spiraling out of control. It's a reaction to symptoms driven by a lack of expertise, discipline, or communication in an organization.

Each phenomenon shared in this book is an opportunity for developing skills, shifting the probability for success just a little bit more in your favor. No one skill or strategy will deliver absolute success. There are no silver bullets here.

HEY, I'M WORKING HERE

Most employers are only interested in employing people when there is work to do. People without work to do are typically promoted to customer status. They will no longer be employed. In the corporate environment, this fact often drives "looking busy" behavior bordering on mania. A full meeting schedule, one hundred emails waiting to be addressed, working ten to twelve hours a day unjustified by output. Delivered value becomes secondary to demonstrable work effort.

The phenomenon observed here: contributors making work more complex and with a higher-than-necessary work content. The stretching of expended efforts, processes, and tasks to appear as overloaded as possible.

There is an element of risk avoidance being demonstrated here. Most likely this is a corporate environment with strict adherence to the N-1 concept shared elsewhere in this book. The slightest hint of slack in the labor supply, and someone is going to be released to pursue other opportunities. Knowing about these risk-avoidance situations and engaging with sensitivity is key. If this is the situation, it is important to not publicly acknowledge it. Instead, try a modified *Distraction Elimination*. Present project tasks without the "filler." Accelerate project execution without upsetting the busy work system perceived as necessary for people to keep their jobs.

This book is about practical project management solutions. Not solving the world's problems. Just accept this kind of survival mechanism will be baked into the company culture and implement a workaround. Subtlety stripping away some of the make-work from specific tasks can accelerate the project without upsetting the greater culture.

Conclusion

Emphasized early in this book is the critical nature of communication proficiency. Familiarity with the strange, less-than-positive communication experiences that manifest in the project management environment is part of the learning experience. Many are addressed by not engaging in them. Others require proactive effort to manage. A few are personal, representing an opportunity for self-improvement.

12

OBSERVED & UNEXPECTED MANAGEMENT PHENOMENA

Engaging management in a project management environment is a requirement, especially for project approval, budgeting, update reporting, scope changes, delays, etc. Addressed here are the people-centric phenomena related to communicating with those in leadership roles. These phenomena may seem obvious to many, but they remain some of the least understood engagement phenomena.

A moment of self-reflection that may help interactions with management is asking yourself if you are someone you would want to manage. Would you want you as a direct report?

> Are you someone you would want to manage?

Presented in this chapter are project management phenomena and sensitive topics around interaction with supervisors and management. Tread lightly and think through a leadership engagement when beginning a skill development path in this space. Gauge where management is at on these concepts. Change management and managing up opportunities abound here.

Engaging management is a requirement for project management. Take the time to develop expertise maximizing the value of those interactions.

Manager's Prerogative

Frogs at the bottom of the well only see part of the sky. – Chinese proverb

---

An insight to keep in mind is that management has more information than you do, and they will not share much of that information with you. This dynamic results in management decisions that at times are a bit opaque. This approach is characteristic of how a hierarchical organization works.

Wasn't there a section in this book on how we are all part of a matrix organization? Now we are back to hierarchy? Regardless of the implementation of the matrix organization, management still follows the hierarchical structure, and information is not widely distributed.

It is likely management did not hire you for your opinion on what management is doing.

The result is perplexing management decisions. They have their reasons, and your approval will not be sought. More will be accomplished by shrugging and rolling with it than by raising your hand and voicing your objections.

Everyone has a boss. Even the CEO reports to a board of directors. With management comes authority and the power to make changes. This includes changing the direction and focus of the organization's efforts. Projects can be altered, often without warning or explanation. Don't take it personally. It is likely someone senior to your manager moved the goalposts. Now your manager has to deal with it. Don't make it difficult. They are probably more frustrated than you are. Support the team and make it happen.

Engaging Management for Success

Nowhere does *Speak the Language* apply more than when communicating with management. Interacting with higher levels of supervision benefits from speaking and writing skills development in profound ways. Appropriate word choice, emphasis, attitude, and credibility become imperative. Poorly worded, incomplete, and inaccurate emails demonstrate a person's limitations to management. Droning on about the topic under discussion does not make someone look smart nor show them as a thought leader. Concise and to the point is the goal (*Forty-Three Seconds*). Demonstrate an understanding that their time is valuable and make efforts to conserve it.

Communicating with more senior members of the organization requires an additional shift in the language used. It is deadly important that what is said or written is accurate (*Perform Due Diligence*), shows teamwork, is positive, and delivers solutions. Senior and executive management are always inspecting the team for effective collaboration, inclusive communication, and constructive paths forward.

Despite what is said about open doors and being there to hear your complaints, management is not interested in your negativity. There is a distinct difference between identifying gaps and presenting constructive solutions versus being the opposite. Identifying genuine challenges is a valuable skill. Complaining, insinuating, grumping, and venting are examples of skills that have no value.

Every manager is presented with a never-ending stream of challenges. They all develop a technique of classifying, organizing, delegating, and then dealing with the most relevant ones. Can you help management achieve their goals without making things worse? Without burning bridges? Without forcing the leadership to micromanage? Can you be trusted with responsibility?

Management Loves Surprises!

No, they do not.

With management, surprises are not good. They happen, but a worthy goal is to avoid making management the last ones aware. Develop the foresight to know when to update your supervisor on a potential issue. The skill of intuitively realizing who needs to know what and when will save everyone unnecessary grief.

A twist on this is the need to communicate information that your supervisor need not take immediate action on. This is not being a snitch or ratting people out. There is information with long-term consequences management may not have visibility to. It takes a judgment call as to whether to share or not.

Managers are adept at recognizing the difference between constructive, forward-looking insights and those trying to use them to advance a personal agenda. They can differentiate between the passive-aggressive efforts of those giving the manager insight into the broader organization. It is a judgement call to determine if a supervisor can handle the responsibility.

Taking stock of how to categorize information and developing the skills to mitigate preventable management surprises are worthy goals. Your project management efforts can only benefit.

PHENOMENAL COSMIC POWER

The phenomenon shared here is how there is an untapped source of resources available to project managers who can present what is needed to leadership in a form those leaders can act on. (*Speak the Language*)

Management comes with responsibility and authority. There is also power associated with management roles. That power is only available for the manager to express in a limited number of conditions. Using power has its own challenges, and HR does not want lawsuits. Having power but no path to use it can be a source of frustration for many managers. They have the tools of power to make decisions and direct action, but unfortunately, those opportunities can be few and far between.

When bringing an opportunity to leadership, present a well-defined ask with a clear, concise, high-value proposition (*Show Me the Money!*). Then place *The Easy Button* in front of them.

HIGH-ENERGY: USEFUL SUPERPOWER OR POTENTIAL KRYPTONITE?

There are times in a project where the path forward is to not make any changes. Just let the contributors execute. The project is in a good place, and the project manager can focus on engagement and maintaining focus. The phenomenon here is that this is almost impossible for high-energy people. They have a compulsion to do something, and that includes endlessly making project changes.

The corporate ideal description for employees often has a high energy requirement. After all, who wants low-energy contributors for their project. The high-energy approach is logical. There are phenomena associated with this personality characteristic, though. High-energy people often enjoy executing at a fast pace and have a "more is better" outlook. There are times when the best course of action is to do nothing. Just let the contributors do their work. High-energy people are challenged in these situations. They are compelled to do something. This is where *Stop Touching Things!* can be seen. A well-planned and managed project will have periods of time where work is progressing and no action from the project manager is needed. Hard to believe, but it happens. Instead of distracting diligent contributors from a running project, use these rare breaks in the action to focus elsewhere. The goal here is awareness. How to react when everything is running smoothly. Recognize the situation and act without disturbing success.

SENSATION OF FORWARD MOTION

The phenomenon of *Sensation of Forward Motion* is obvious but often not part of project planning. Project managers will often focus on delivering that one big thing. This is a mistake because there will be long pauses between anything being seen as completed. Nothing will get management more interested in your project than the perception that progress is not occurring. There are two strategies to prevent this potentially unconstructive scrutiny. Leverage completing short, quick parts of the project and provide regular updates. Don't just work on the big parts of the project. Deliver on shorter, straightforward efforts. This creates a sensation of progress. This is soothing for management.

The next part is to have semi-regular updates to management on progress. This has synergy with the short effort completion. Together, these lower the probability management will panic inspect the project. A key point here: integrity. Don't make up progress. Everything must be above board because at some point someone may make a detailed review.

THE HURRY UP MYTH

> No one wants to fly in an airplane
> hurriedly put together.

This is the fraternal twin to *Switching Losses Are Not a Figment of Your Imagination*. Perhaps there are roles out there where the opportunity to work slowly is part of the culture. For the rest of us, there is one speed. The request will come in to shorten the delivery time. Move faster and hurry up. This request does not make sense. People are working, and asking them to *work faster* will only inject issues. The likely reason for the hurry-up request is to increase tension with the hope it increases engagement, focus, and subsequent productivity.

It may be an option to put aside other, unrelated tasks and focus exclusively on the one effort. This assumes that there are no delays while awaiting delivery of some needed component, or the results of testing, or the product of other contributors' work. Asking people to hurry up, increases the likelihood of critical aspects of the projects being overlooked. The other problem with hurry up is nobody knows how to do it. Much like how self-organizing teams are a fallacy, it is unlikely individuals or groups who are requested to hurry up will deliver. The more likely outcome is confusion, delays, and added work.

> ## The infuriating cousin to "Hurry up," is "Just a little bit more."

The other, more infuriating cousin to hurry up is just a little bit more. Saying this is not a big request; it is just a little bit more effort.

Hurry up and just a little bit more are undisciplined approaches that should never be brought into the project management environment.

Unrealized assets

An unfinished project is an unrealized asset. Investing time and resources in chartering a project, executing on a project, and then not delivering is dereliction on the part of the project manager, representing failure. The unrealized asset is not just the hard assets purchased for a project and left incomplete. Nor is it the cost of the contributor's efforts that never come to fruition. The real loss is in the opportunity cost. What was the expected value from delivering a complete project? Or from another project if the resources had been applied to completion? What could have been accomplished if all the contributors' efforts had been applied to something that was completed?

No one puts money into opportunities to then receive no return on investment and have their originally invested money forgotten. This is what happens when projects are not completed.

There is a psychological impact as well. Contributors derive satisfaction and professional development from completing tasks contributing to project success. Projects that never deliver deny them this experience. This will negatively impact future efforts.

Project managers are not just responsible for project execution. They are responsible for the money spent, contributor cost, opportunity cost of the money spent and contributor time, and the ROI the project is to deliver.

Management Cannot Value Something They Do Not Understand

Be mindful of how actions taken are being perceived. In a complex work environment, project execution can be open to interpretation. A common project characteristic that will bring management attention is the order in which tasks are performed or why a task is not a priority. If the why is not obvious there will be questions. If the optics are less than constructive (*Perception is Reality*), perhaps there is an opportunity for preemptive clarification and managing of expectations. Don't let negative perceptions escalate due to a lack of sensitivity and a straightforward explanation. And don't expect management to simply understand on their own. Effort must be invested in project messaging to guide perception.

Not Important, Useful

At some point in a project manager's journey, they may find themselves being categorized as useful. Perhaps being useful is the result of the progression of project management skills and experience. Useful people are often mistaken for being important. It is not uncommon for useful people to be directly tasked by important people with important efforts. Important people are comfortable delegating to useful people. Useful people may, temporarily, wield authority and power due to the situation. They also know better than to abuse the situation or think that they are now important.

> Your reward for good work is more work.

Management loves useful people. Useful people are those who consistently deliver while requiring minimal maintenance. When a project manager is useful, their project efforts enjoy a high level of support. Useful people work on interesting things and get to accomplish a lot. The downside is that useful people are very busy and are tasked heavily. Much of what is assigned will have high visibility. The difficulty level will be high, and performance punishment is often a result. Useful is a good place to be. Learn to be useful.

THE EASY BUTTON

This phenomenon is the key to *Phenomenal Cosmic Powers*. A *Speak the Language* approach that increases success, *The Easy Button* is presenting to leadership a carefully crafted opportunity to remove obstacles or increase project velocity. The goal is to share an opportunity with leadership that is as friction-free as possible to accept. *The Easy Button* is also useful for contributors for buy-in to a different approach. There are two potential sides to the easy button, organizational and rational.

The organizational easy button is delivered without unnecessary complexity. Plan out addressing frustrating delays and misunderstandings before they occur. Organize project information, ask questions and get answers, and process details ahead of time (*Now Can You Explain It?*). Get approvals in advance; remove obstacles.

The rational easy button is about reducing injected stress. Address contributors' *Liability, the Project Killer* up front. Run interference on political aspects. The value of what is included in the rational easy button changes from person to person. A custom-tailored approach addressing individual needs can be advantageous here. Any effort to rationalize project execution is generally welcomed. Building the easy button is a demonstration of competence, and project participants appreciate this (*Credibility*).

A popular response to a well-delivered easy button: "That is all you need?" Leadership and contributors are often genuinely surprised when they encounter this approach. It offers them a straightforward ask that allows them to efficiently accomplish something while demonstrating their competency. All leading to a shot of effort accomplished endorphins at project end.

Having project tasks prioritized and defined in advance is important. It's the proverbial easy button. Everyone wants to work with the easy button. Be the easy button. Like a glass of cool water in a desert, the easy button is received especially well by those frustrated by politics and complexity (*N-1*, *matrix*).

HOW LAZINESS CAN BE USEFUL

There is a quote about how lazy managers find the most efficient path to completing a task. Lazy, in this context, is not the common use of this word. Instead, it refers to an individual who is efficient with the energy available. This is a worthwhile skill, as resources are always in short supply. Lazy people question expending effort. The useful aspect of laziness is looking at a task and being willing to question "why." Why should we do this? Why this way? Is there a better way that takes up less time or resources?

The lazy approach frees up bandwidth and resources for other opportunities. Having a limited few hard-working, lazy people in the organization is a force multiplier. Laziness is intolerance of inefficiency and of solutions lacking elegance or insight. Lazy people are fundamentally skeptical.

The corporate poster child for success is an extroverted, high-energy, constantly in motion go-getter, continuously taking action. They must be seen doing things at all times. That kind of personality is not sensitive to opportunities to use less energy. There instead is a tendency toward working harder, not less. Overcoming challenges by expending more energy. In an environment populated with these energetic, hard-working, driven managers fearlessly engaging difficult challenges to prove their value, a lazy manager will find a target-rich environment of low-hanging, easily delivered value.

Not everything has to be that hard. Sometimes it is easy.

Conclusion

A project manager's quality of management engagement is critical to project success. It is also critical to a project manager's career success. This chapter presented multiple people-centric phenomena directly related to interacting with management and promoting project excellence.

Messaging for project progress, value, and opportunities for improvement is a core project manager responsibility. Understand how the leadership perceives value. How money is analyzed. Bottom-line contribution? Top line growth? ROI or NPV? Know these characteristics of the organization and *Speak the Language*.

PULLING IT ALL TOGETHER

Did we learn anything?

There are several key takeaways to land with the reader. A good place to start is that communications, written and verbal, are important to project management success. Any incremental improvement in engaging contributors and leadership will occur only from communication. The probability of success in this space will depend heavily on the communication capabilities of the project manager. Knowing how to engage the project, contributors, and leadership are important skills. Communication is the vehicle that facilitates engagement efforts. Knowing who, when, and about what is the path forward.

Paying attention to what project aspects contributors are engaged with or focused upon is an everyday effort. Defining focus, advocating for focus, and assessing the current state of contributors' focus are important for every project. Knowing these gives the project manager visibility into where the project is developing towards. If the current state of focus is not meeting expectations, then the project manager must engage, through communications, the pertinent parties and adjust accordingly.

Keeping contributors engaged and focused requires the application of tension. Meetings to discuss progress and regular inspection of deliverables are tension creators. Communicating with all involved parties builds a subconscious impression that someone is paying attention. This impression is not accomplished with weekly meetings or unemotionally checking boxes on a spreadsheet. *Get on It. Stay on It.* creates that tension. This means demonstrating interest and the application of an appropriate amount of energy.

When communications, engagement, focus, and tension fail, having a planned *Defined Escalation* approach ready is critical. This is the single most important, engagement process necessary to decrease project friction. Reluctant, or difficult contributors are a fact of life for a project manager. Having this process pre-approved by leadership and at the ready will make these inevitable interactions less stressful. A developed, neutral approach to align contributors is a beautiful thing.

Tension is a strange concept. It must be delivered in the correct amount. Too much tension risks negative outcomes from contributors. Too little tension and engagement and focus suffer. The best tension analogy is from fishing. Once the fish is on the hook, tension is maintained to keep it there. Sometimes only the lightest pull, is needed just enough to keep reeling in the fish. Once a project is in motion, the project manager needs to keep tension on all aspects of the project. The tension requirement is situational. Some aspects may require daily inspection. Other contributors are self-starters and will drive forward with minimal supervision.

All communication, engagement, focus, and tension efforts involve people. This is where the people-centric project management phenomena become part of the project effort. Knowing they exist and having some idea on how to *Prevent, Ignore, Mitigate, or Leverage* each of these is a project manager's secret weapon.

Knowledge of the existence of people-centric project management phenomena is not common. Many will suspect the existence of some of them. More experienced project managers will recognize and have techniques for engaging certain more prominent ones. The fundamental disconnect shared here is the non-intuitive nature of the phenomena.

The individual occurrences are often difficult to recognize in real time without prior understanding. The fact that there are so many of them is a surprise to most.

> People-centric phenomena skills can be combined to achieve synergistic outcomes.

Visibility to the concept and types of these phenomena opens up a constellation of project acceleration opportunities. Quality improvement and project friction reduction at little to no cost, other than the self-improvement of reading this book. All with no capital expenditure, only individual skill development. This in-between space in every project is waiting to be addressed.

Near-zero cost delivering unlimited growth

Acknowledgement of the phenomena, followed by skill development improves a project manager's abilities in navigating the human equation and executing larger/longer and more complex efforts. With experience, anticipating phenomena will become second nature. Preventing what in the past would have brought your project management efforts to a standstill.

After the flagship concepts of communications, engagement, focus, and tension are part of a project manager's toolbox, then it is time to look to the next loosely grouped concepts of project planning/execution, process, and adjacent topics.

If there was a wanted poster for worst phenomenon, it would probably be *Angels on a pinhead*. There are others to be found in the project planning/execution chapters, such as *The ABCDE incidence*.

From a lesson in tension standpoint, *Balls in a Tube* is where significant short-term gains can be found.

Process phenomena are almost never addressed upfront in a constructive way. They are always *In-Flight Missile Repairman* situations. Process viability is never discussed before a project launches. Inspecting critical processes before the project begins is probably wishful thinking. But, were it to happen, just imagine the benefits!

Then there are the project- and process-adjacent phenomena such as timeframe, people being people, and the dreaded matrix/N-1 impacts. Everyone handles social aspects differently. What is shared here is how personalities can and will impact project execution and quality.

Project efficiency and quality are also impacted by matrix/N-1 implementation. Yes, human resource strategies impact project management success. Most project managers will have no say in matrix/N-1 strategies. However, having visibility to the eccentricities driven into project execution due to HR policies may make project planning more manageable.

Success breeds success (*Credibility*). A track record of meeting project expectations makes future efforts easier. Build those skills, and as a project manager improves, contributors will accept collaboration more readily. This mutual synergy becomes a win-win for everyone. Project efficiency and quality improvement due to past successes.

> A track record of meeting project expectations make future efforts easier.

While lists, Gantt charts, and project management tools are not topics discussed in this book, they are useful when used properly. The insight shared here is that people use those tools. And if the complexities of human beings are not taken into account, the project will not process and tool its way to success. If you are going to play, play to win. In project management, the project managers and their skills—especially in the people space—are key to success.

THE PHENOMENA

GLOSSARY OF TERMS & NOTES ON ORGANIZATION

This glossary has been included here to establish a common understanding of the fundamentals.

The Project Management Toolbox – The chapters listed in the index are semi-organized into relatively associated groupings. These chapter groupings are not absolute and, much like the tools in a toolbox, can be selectively utilized as needed. Hence the reference to the chapters and their listed phenomena as being in "The Toolbox."

People-centric – Focus on the human part of the equation. This does not include checklists or software applications. Leveraging understanding of why and how people behave when executing tasks.

Project Management Phenomena – Repeating people, process, and project interactions not commonly understood. The phenomenon (singular) / phenomena (plural) concept is woven into every part of this book.

Icons to help clarify the focus of each section:
Each people-centric phenomenon is denoted with:

The Matrix organization – An organizational philosophy where the hierarchy is flattened and related skills and resources are grouped together. The goal is to reduce cost and facilitate outsourcing.

N-1 and the stretch – A human resources philosophy implemented to increase productivity. The number of people to perform a task is identified. Then one is subtracted from that number (N-1). The attenuated team is then assigned the task. The goal is a "close enough" labor supply that the people "stretch" their efforts to cover the gap.
Most employers implement both the matrix and N-1 philosophies. Even smaller organizations where these practices are not official policy still do this.

Italics references – There will be cross-references called out as they are relevant. Example: (*Words Matter*). These indicate phenomena that are relevant to the discussion. Due to the number (50+) of the phenomena discussed in this book and their interrelated nature, they may be referenced out of sequence.

Phenomenon combos – Phenomenon are often experienced in combinations. Example - *Forty-Three Seconds + Asking Good Questions + Now Can You Explain It*

Critical thinking – The objective analysis and evaluation of an issue in order to form a judgment; Self-guided, self-disciplined thinking that attempts to reason at the highest level of quality in a fair-minded way. The kind of thinking in which you question, analyze, interpret, evaluate and make a judgement about what you read, hear, say, or write.

Asker of impertinent questions – The willingness to inspect deeper regardless of social skepticism

Inset paragraphs are stories shared to better explain the origins and character of the phenomena being discussed in that section.

Spaghetti organization – Many of the concepts and approaches shared here have a relationship to each other and have been organized accordingly. Others are part of a constellation of tools and presented in loose groupings.

ABOUT THE AUTHOR

Erik Lange is a technician, engineer, prolific author, and asker of impertinent questions living in Jackson, WI, with his wife and their dog, Winnie.